GEOLOGY
THE ACTIVE EARTH

Other Titles in *Ranger Rick's NatureScope*

Ranger Rick's NatureScope

GEOLOGY
THE ACTIVE EARTH

National Wildlife Federation

LEARNING
TRIANGLE
PRESS

*Connecting
kids, parents, and teachers
through learning*

An imprint of McGraw-Hill
New York San Francisco Washington, D.C. Auckland Bogotá Caracas
Lisbon London Madrid Mexico City Milan Montreal New Delhi
San Juan Singapore Sydney Tokyo Toronto

McGraw-Hill

A Division of The **McGraw·Hill** *Companies*

NATIONAL WILDLIFE FEDERATION®

1 2 3 4 5 6 7 8 9 0 JDL/JDL 9 0 2 1 0 9 8 7

ISBN 0-07-046511-8

NatureScope® was originally conceived by National Wildlife Federation's School Programs Editorial Staff, under the direction of Judy Braus, Editor. Special thanks to all of the Editorial Staff, Scientific, Educational Consultants and Contributors who brought this series of eighteen publications to life.

NATIONAL WILDLIFE FEDERATION EDITORIAL STAFF
Creative Services Manager: Sharon Schiliro
Editor, Ranger Rick® magazine: Gerry Bishop
Director Classroom–related Programs: Margaret Tunstall
Contributors: Carol Boggis, Rhonda Lucas Donald, Sharon Levy, Susan Makurat–Bond

McGRAW-HILL EDP STAFF
Acquisitions Editor: Judith Terrill-Breuer
Editing Supervisor: Patricia V. Amoroso
Production Supervisor: Claire B. Stanley
Designer: Jaclyn J. Boone
Cover Design: David Saylor

RRNS

MEETING THE CHALLENGE

GOAL

Ranger Rick's Nature-Scope is a creative education series dedicated to inspiring in children an understanding and appreciation of the natural world while developing the skills they will need to make responsible decisions about the environment.

I t has been almost a decade since the publication of the first *Geology: The Active Earth* in the **Ranger Rick's NatureScope** series. Since that time, we have had both encouraging and discouraging news about the environment. Our awareness has been heightened and much has been done, but there is still much to do.

One of the best ways to ensure sustained concern for our planet and the creatures who inhabit it is to educate our children. This new edition of *Geology: The Active Earth* brings to the classroom the original material which has survived the test of time, along with new essays by and about people working in the field today, people who are still learning about how our environment works and who are taking action to preserve it. Here also is the sense of wonder they feel as they work in the natural world. This new edition also includes an updated bibliography for further study and enrichment.

The effort to save wildlife and habitat will span many generations. Like all lifelong commitments, there is no better time to begin than when we are young.

National Wildlife Federation

TABLE OF CONTENTS

A Close-Up Look At Geology: The Active Earth

L ooking at the Table of Contents, you can see we've divided *Geology: The Active Earth* into five chapters (each of which deals with a broad geology theme) and an appendix. Each of the five chapters includes *background information* that explains concepts and vocabulary, *activities* that relate to the chapter theme, and *Copycat Pages* that reinforce many of the concepts introduced in the activities.

You can choose single activity ideas or teach each chapter as a unit. Either way, each activity stands by itself and includes teaching objectives, a list of materials needed, suggested age groups, subjects covered, and a step-by-step explanation of how to do the activity. (The objectives, materials, age groups, and subjects are highlighted in the left-hand margin for easy reference.)

Age Groups
The suggested age groups are:
- Primary (grades K-2)
- Intermediate (grades 3-5)
- Advanced (grades 6-7)

Each chapter usually begins with primary activities and ends with intermediate or advanced activities. But don't feel bound by the grade levels we suggest. Resourceful teachers, naturalists, parents, and club leaders can adapt most of these activities to fit their particular age group and needs.

Outdoor Activities
The best way to learn about geology is to step outside and study the Earth around you. Outdoor activities are coded in this issue with this symbol:

Copycat Pages
The *Copycat Pages* supplement the activities and include ready-to-copy games, puzzles, coloring pages, and/or worksheets. *Answers to all Copycat Pages are in the texts of the activities.*

What's At The End
The last section, the *Appendix*, is loaded with reference suggestions that include books, films, maps, and where to get rock and mineral samples. It also has suggestions of where to get more geology information.

EARTH ON THE MOVE

As you read this sentence, Africa is being torn apart from Asia, a new mountain range is being shoved up in the Mediterranean, the Red Sea is well on its way to becoming an ocean, and the Pacific Ocean is shrinking. But don't worry. All these events are happening so slowly that during our lifetime we won't even notice the changes.

A hundred years ago many geologists would have scoffed at the idea of moving continents and shrinking oceans. But today most accept the theory that continents, as well as the entire crust of the Earth, are "on the move." In this chapter we'll look at the structure of the Earth and how forces inside the Earth help power the changes we see on the surface.

THE EARTH, INSIDE AND OUT

Since the early 1900s, geologists have known that the Earth is divided into three main layers: a thin outer *crust,* a thicker *mantle,* and a *core.* But exactly how these layers interact and what they are made of are still open to debate.

The crust is the only layer that geologists can really study first-hand. So geologists have had to study other data, such as the path earthquake shock waves take as they travel through the Earth, to find out more about the mantle and core. Starting with the crust, here's a closer look at each layer:

A Thin Skin: The outermost layer of the Earth—the layer we walk on—is a thin, rocky skin that covers the planet. In relation to the Earth, this crust is about as thin as a postage stamp stuck on a billiard ball. At its thickest, which is under mountain ranges, the crust is only about 22 miles (35 km) thick—about 1/200th of the Earth's diameter.

By comparing rock samples dredged from the ocean floor with those on the continents, scientists found there were two distinct types of crust: *continental crust* and *oceanic crust.* Continental crust makes up the continents and contains light-colored rocks (such as granite) composed mainly of the elements aluminum, silicon, and oxygen. This layer of crust is much thicker than the oceanic crust, which forms the ocean floor. Although the oceanic crust is thinner, it is made of denser rocks (such as basalt) containing the elements iron, magnesium, silicon, and oxygen. Because of the difference in densities, the lighter continental crust "floats" higher on the underlying mantle than does the oceanic crust.

The Movin' Mantle: Underneath the crust is the much denser mantle. Although no one has ever drilled into the mantle, geologists think it is made up of many of the same elements that form the crust. (The mantle is hotter and denser than the crust because the temperature and pressure inside the Earth increase as the depth increases.)

Although most of the mantle is made up of solid rock, geologists think it is composed of several zones. The uppermost zone, the area lying directly underneath the crust, is cooler and thus more rigid than the lower parts of the mantle. This thin, uppermost layer of the mantle, combined with the thin, rocky crust, forms a rigid layer of rock called the *lithosphere* (see diagram on page 9).

Below the lithosphere geologists think there is a hot, weak zone that is also solid, but can "flow" at a very, very slow rate. This weaker zone is called the *asthenosphere.* Geologists think the lithosphere "floats" on this more mobile zone in the mantle, and slides around on it very slowly. *(continued next page)*

3

Diagram 1

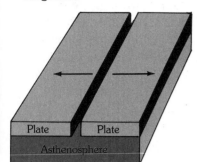

Two plates move
apart.

Diagram 2

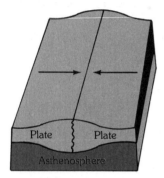

Two plates collide.

Many geologists are convinced that strong convection currents exist within the mantle. (Convection is the process by which hot material rises to the surface, spreads and cools, and then sinks again, like soup being heated in a saucepan.) These convection currents, which geologists think are fueled by heat given off by the core and some radioactive decay in the mantle, constantly transfer heat from the deep mantle to the crust at a very slow rate.

Heavy Metal: Deep within the Earth is the core—a mass of hot, heavy metals (mostly iron and nickel) that sank, due to gravity, after the Earth formed. The core is almost twice as dense as the mantle and appears to be the main source of heat that triggers the convection currents in the mantle. Geologists know that the core is made up of two very different layers. The *outer core* is molten and is responsible for the Earth's magnetic field. And the *inner core* is solid.

PLATES ON THE MOVE

So what does the inside of the Earth have to do with changes on the surface? Everything! Most geologists think that powerful convection currents in the mantle, driven by heat given off by the core and radioactive decay, are the force behind many of the changes that occur in the crust.

In the 1960s geologists developed an exciting new theory called *plate tectonics*. Plate tectonics proposes that the lithosphere (the crust and uppermost layer of the mantle) is not a continuous sheet of solid rock. Instead it is divided into about 12 enormous plates and many smaller plates that "float" like icebergs on the top of the asthenosphere. These plates, which can be hundreds or thousands of miles across, move relative to one another and they carry the continents and ocean basins with them as they drift about. For example, most of North America and a good part of the Atlantic Ocean are on the North American Plate. But Hawaii, part of California and Alaska, and most of the Pacific Ocean are part of the Pacific Plate.

Slippin' and Slidin': Plate tectonics revolutionized geology because it finally explained how most major geological events occur. Geologists could see that most mountain building and earthquake and volcanic activity take place along the margins of the plates. And as they studied the ways plates interact with each other, they found that in some areas new crust is always forming, while in other areas old crust is constantly being destroyed. Here's a look at the main ways plates interact with each other to influence the crust:

- **Oozing Crust:** New oceanic crust is formed at oceanic rifts, where two plates pull apart from each other. Magma (hot, molten rock from deep in the Earth) oozes out from cracks along these rifts and hardens to form new crust. (When magma reaches the surface of the Earth, it is called *lava*.)

    This *ocean-floor spreading* is occurring in all the world's major oceans. For example, new crust is constantly oozing out of the the Mid-Atlantic Ridge that separates the North American Plate from the Eurasian Plate. For the last 250 million years, as new crust has been added to each plate, Europe has been slowly pushed away from North America, and the Atlantic Ocean has gotten wider (see diagram 1).

- **Crash!:** Just as some plates are moving away from each other, others are moving toward each other. When two plates carrying continents run into each other, the collision usually crumples the leading edge of both plates and creates lofty mountain ranges over a period of millions of years. For example, the Himalayas were formed when the plate carrying India collided with the plate carrying Eurasia (see diagram 2).

- **Bye, Bye, Plate:** Old plates never die, they just subduct. If two plates collide and one is made up of continental crust and the other is made up of oceanic

Diagram 3

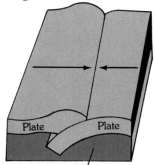

One plate subducts beneath another.

Diagram 4

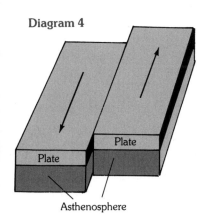

Two plates slide past each other.

Recently geophysicists have discovered that transitions of matter, from one kind of solid to another kind, in the Earth's mantle can set off *deep earthquakes*. The largest deep earthquake ever recorded—398 miles (640 km) under the ground—occurred in Bolivia in June 1994.

crust, a deep trench forms in the ocean floor as the denser oceanic plate bends down and slides under, or *subducts* beneath, the edge of the other plate. The pressure of this movement crumples the leading edge of the upper plate, creating mountain ranges such as the Andes along the margin. As the lower plate is pushed under, it begins to heat up in the hotter mantle. And eventually the ocean sediment on the plate begins to melt. This melted rock, or magma, from the subducted plate is less dense than the mantle rock and begins to move upward, often fueling volcanoes in the mountain ranges that have formed on the upper plate. For example, the volcanic region of the Pacific Northwest, which includes Mount St. Helens, is the result of plate subduction (see diagram 3).

- **Just Scraping By:** Sometimes two plates slide sideways past each other, as the Pacific and North American Plates are doing along California's San Andreas Fault. (A *fault* is a break in the Earth's crust caused by stresses that are usually related to plate movements.) This slipping motion often causes earthquakes, but neither plate is destroyed in the sideways slippage (see diagram 4).
- **Underwater Torches:** In some places, a narrow plume of hot material rises up through the mantle and creates a *hotspot* under the plate. The extra heat melts some of the mantle rock, which makes its way up through the plate to form a volcano. As the plate slowly moves over the stationary hotspot, a line of volcanoes is formed. (Once a volcano drifts past a hotspot, it becomes inactive. But a new, active volcano will form over the hotspot.) Some geologists think a hotspot under the Pacific Ocean formed the Hawaiian Islands.

SHAKE, RATTLE, AND ROLL

Most of the changes in the Earth's crust are so slow, they go unnoticed. But a few are so violent, they rock the planet and threaten life. Two of the most dramatic results of plate movement are earthquakes and volcanoes.

Magma on the Move: Volcanoes usually form along plate boundaries. What a volcano looks like and exactly what will come pouring out of it depend on where and how it forms. For example, where plates are moving apart as in the Mid-Atlantic Ridge, a very liquid type of lava called basalt oozes out of undersea volcanoes. This basalt hardens into "pillows" and flat sheets of new crust. But where plates of the crust are colliding, the lava is much thicker and often creates violent eruptions as trapped gases explode and shatter the pasty lava to bits. This is what happened when Mount St. Helens erupted in May, 1980.

Rockin' and Rollin': Earthquakes can happen anywhere on the Earth, but just like volcanoes, most occur along plate margins. For example, ocean ridges are earthquake zones, although the earthquakes that occur there are usually too small and too far from land to do much damage to the continents. Earthquakes also occur along subduction zones and along boundaries where plates are slipping past each other. These earthquakes are often the largest, most destructive ones.

During an earthquake, the ground shakes violently for a few moments and then stops. (Large earthquakes can shake the ground for several minutes, although most of the shaking is usually felt for less than 30 seconds.) This shaking is caused by stresses in the crust that cause sudden slippage on fault surfaces. The stresses build up because plate movements are not smooth or continuous. Instead, the plates get "caught" on one another and remain stuck until the forces pushing the two plates toward or past each other cause them to bend like a bow. When they can no longer resist the strain, the plates suddenly break apart, ending up in a less stressed position. As they do this, shock waves rapidly travel out from the *focus*—the place where the rocks snapped apart. Surface waves are most intense and damaging at the *epicenter,* the point on the Earth's surface directly above the focus. (See pages 8 and 11 for more about earthquakes.)

A Quakin', Shakin' Earth

Take a look at some of the violent ways the Earth changes and at the effects these events can have.

Objective:
Discuss volcanoes, earthquakes, tsunamis, and geysers.

Ages:
Primary, Intermediate, and Advanced

Materials:
- *copies of pages 13, 14, and 15*
- *pictures of tsunamis, earthquakes, volcanoes, and geysers (optional)*
- *scissors*
- *glue*
- *construction paper*
- *crayons or markers*
- *rulers, yardsticks, or measuring tape*
- *stopwatch*
- *clock with second hand*
- *chalk*
- *blacktop area*
- *flag or other marker*
- *stapler*

Subject:
Science

Unless you've seen a volcanic eruption or experienced an intense earthquake, it's hard to comprehend the incredible forces that exist within the Earth. In this two-part activity your kids can find out more about some of these "earth-shaking" events.

PART 1: PICTURE BOOKS

Before you get started, make your own picture book by following the directions below. Then, using the picture book and the information on pages 4, 5, and 8, discuss with the children what earthquakes, volcanoes, tsunamis, and geysers are. As you explain each type of event, turn the center flap of the appropriate picture in your picture book to show them what these events can be like. You might also want to show them other pictures of these events. Be sure to explain that violent geological events are rare, but when they

do happen they can cause a lot of damage. You might also mention that in the last few decades, geologists have learned a lot about how and why these events occur. And as we learn more, we will be better able to minimize the damage to human life and property.

Afterward pass out copies of pages 14 and 15, scissors, glue, construction paper, and crayons or markers and let the kids create their own earth-shaking picture pages.

HOW TO MAKE A PICTURE BOOK

1. Color the pictures on pages 14 and 15.

2. Cut out all of the pictures on both sheets along *the solid lines only*. Then fold each one in half so that the drawing is to the *inside* (see diagram).

3. Match each numbered "before" picture from page 14 with the lettered "after" picture on page 15 that goes with it and lay each match down side by side. (For example, picture 1 goes with picture A.) Then glue the back of the right half of the numbered picture to the back of the left half of the lettered picture (see diagram). With younger kids you might want to work together as a group doing one pair at a time.

4. When all of the pictures are glued to their matches, have the kids use the pictures to make a book. Just have them stack three pieces of construction paper together, fold them in half, and staple them along the fold. Then they can glue a finished picture onto each sheet of the book, label each disaster, and draw their own picture on the cover.

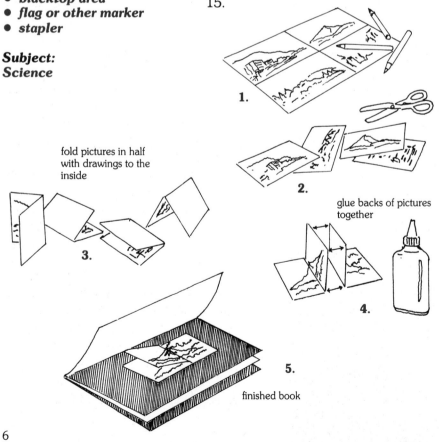

fold pictures in half with drawings to the inside

1.

2.

glue backs of pictures together

3.

4.

5.

finished book

PART 2: SHAKE, RATTLE, AND ROLL

Begin by using the information on pages 4, 5, and 8 to talk about earthquakes, volcanoes, tsunamis, and geysers. Then pass out copies of page 13 to the group and read over the earth-shaking trivia.

After you've looked at the page, ask the kids if they can imagine how big a tsunami is or how far the plates shifted in the San Francisco earthquake in 1906. Then tell them they'll be doing some short activities to help them understand how powerful some of these events have been.

Below we've listed some suggestions for these activities. Adapt these suggestions to fit the level of your group.

- **Walloping Waves:** To illustrate the estimated height of the tsunami produced by Krakatoa's explosion, have the kids break into groups of four or five. Each group will figure out the average of their heights and then divide that number into 100 feet (30 m) to find out how many "average" kids it would take to "stand up to" the tsunami. (One hundred feet [30 m] is about the same height as a 10-story building!)
- **Rockin' and Rollin' Ground:** Move outside and have the kids form two lines facing each other. Tell them that they represent the two plates on either side of the San Andreas Fault in California. Have one child join hands with the person opposite him or her and explain that they represent a fence that stretches across the fault. On your signal, have the two lines take ten sideways steps in opposite directions. The "fence" should stretch and finally break during the shift.

  Explain that this kind of shift occurred in the San Francisco earthquake

of 1906, when the plates shifted a record 20 feet (6 m). Fences, bridges, roads, and buildings that reached across the fault were broken apart as the plates shifted.

- **Racing an Avalanche:** Have the kids line up, then place a marker 100 feet (30 m) away. Explain that they'll be trying to run faster than the hot mud and ash that flowed down Mount St. Helens' slopes after its 1980 eruption. Give the signal and time the kids as they run to the marker.

  When they catch their breath, tell them that they were all beaten by the avalanche. It sped down the mountain at about 100 miles (160 km) per hour and would have finished the race in less than one second! (Point out to the kids that not all lava, mud, and other material ejected from volcanoes flow this fast.)
- **Floating Boulders:** Next move to a blacktop area and pass out chalk to the kids. Tell them that rocks up to 10 feet (3 m) long were blasted out of the crater when Krakatoa exploded. Because they were *pumice* (hardened lava with many air holes), these rocks floated and were a hazard for ships long after the explosion. Have the kids measure and draw 10-foot (3-m) rocks with chalk on the blacktop.
- **Timed Quakes:** Divide the kids into pairs and have one person in each pair keep time while the other one shakes. Tell the "shakers" they should shake until they think one minute is up. Were they right? Then have the kids switch roles. Afterward tell the kids that most earthquakes last for less than one minute, but a severe earthquake in Alaska in 1964 shook the ground for several minutes.
- **A Blast from the Past:** When Mount Vesuvius erupted in AD 79, it covered the city of Herculaneum with a layer of mud 60 feet (18 m) deep. Have the kids figure out the height of your school (one story is about 10 feet [3 m] high) and see how many times the school could fit inside this layer of mud.

(continued next page)

Luise Woelflein

7

SOME EARTH-SHAKING FACTS

Tsunamis

A tsunami is a giant ocean wave that starts when a sudden motion in the Earth jolts and displaces the water in the ocean. Undersea earthquakes, coastal earthquakes, and volcanic activity are the usual causes of tsunamis. Most tsunamis occur in the Pacific Ocean.

The height and speed of a tsunami are affected by the depth of the water it is traveling through. Out in the middle of the ocean, a tsunami may be only three feet (90 cm) high, but when it reaches shore it may tower above land 100 feet (30 m) or more.

Volcanoes

A volcano is one or more deep openings, or *vents,* in the surface of the Earth through which molten rock, gases, solid material (such as ash and solid rock), and steam are forced out. The way a volcano erupts depends on the characteristics of the magma, the shape and length of the vents, and whether or not the vents are plugged by rock. For example, some eruptions are very quiet and the lava that flows out is very runny. Other eruptions are violent, flinging out 20-mile (32-km) high columns of ash or forming ash clouds that are loaded with bits of lava.

The type of eruptions a volcano has influences the way it looks. For example, if a volcano usually ejects runny lava, a gently sloping, dome-shaped mountain will form. On the other hand, if a volcano alternately ejects thick lava and ash and cinders, a steep, cone-shaped mountain will form.

Although the eruption of a volcano can be one of the most destructive forces on Earth, volcanoes also build new land, produce mineral-rich ash that helps fertilize the soil, and produce gases that are important to life on Earth.

Earthquakes

Earthquakes can happen anywhere that movement occurs along a fault. But most earthquakes occur near plate boundaries. (See page 5 for more about earthquakes.)

To compare earthquakes, scientists measure each quake's intensity and magnitude. The intensity of an earthquake is a measure of how badly it shakes people and people-made objects. It is measured on the Mercalli Intensity Scale from 1 (only detectable by sensitive instruments) to 12 (causing complete destruction of buildings and other objects). The magnitude of an earthquake is a measure of how much energy an earthquake gives off and is independent of how much damage it causes. Magnitude is recorded by seismographs and is measured on the Richter Scale from about −3 (barely detectable by seismographs) to about 9 (earthquakes that can cause severe damage).

Though a big earthquake can cause a lot of damage, sometimes a greater amount of damage is caused by the fires that rage afterward. As the Earth shakes it often disrupts electrical and gas lines that can, in turn, start fires. And broken water lines make fighting the fires almost impossible.

Geysers

It takes three major things to form a geyser: water, a series of irregularly shaped underground rocky "tubes," and a heat source hot enough to boil water. The water that is shot out of geysers is usually groundwater. (Groundwater originates from rain or snow melt that has trickled deep into the ground through cracks and pores in the rocks.) As this water circulates deep underground it is heated by hot rocks that in turn have been heated by an underlying body of magma.

How often a geyser "blows" and how long its eruption lasts vary from geyser to geyser. Some geysers erupt every hour or so while others may have several hours, days, or weeks between eruptions. And while some geysers may gush for only a few minutes, others may have eruptions that last for 45 minutes or more.

Almost all of the world's geysers are in New Zealand, Iceland, and Yellowstone National Park in Wyoming. Yellowstone has approximately 200 geysers—more than the rest of the world combined!

geyser

- When a severe underwater quake is recorded, a tsunami alert is sent out to all vulnerable coastlines. However, because tsunamis travel very fast, reaching 600 miles an hour, warnings do not always arrive on time.

- Tsunami waves have reached more than 200 feet in height and have traveled all the way across the Pacific Ocean.

The Earth, Inside and Out

As a group, act out the structure of the Earth, then make models of the Earth's layers.

Objective:
Describe the structure of the Earth.

Ages:
Intermediate and Advanced

Materials:
- *chalkboard or easel paper*
- *scissors*
- *slips of paper*
- *small cardboard boxes*
- *small plastic Ziplock bags*
- *clay*
- *masking tape*
- *watercolors or poster paints*
- *paintbrushes*
- *materials for making dough (see recipe at end of activity)*
- *red food coloring*
- *water*
- *cardboard*
- *glue*
- *construction paper*
- *plastic wrap (optional)*

Subject:
Science

I n this activity the kids in your group can learn about the structure of the Earth by building a human Earth. Afterward they can make their own smaller Earth models. Before you get started, copy the diagram below onto a chalkboard or sheet of easel paper. Also copy these words onto separate slips of paper and put them into a hat (you should end up with 30 slips):

inner core (1)
outer core (3)
deep mantle (6)
asthenosphere (8)
lithosphere (12)

(Adjust the numbers to fit the size of your group.)

Begin by showing the kids the diagram you copied earlier. Explain that the Earth has three main layers: crust, mantle, and core. Also explain that the mantle and core are divided into different "sub-layers." Then, using the background information on pages 3-4, discuss each layer and sublayer of the Earth. (*Note:* We are calling the area of the mantle below the asthenosphere the *deep mantle.*)

Next take the kids to a large open area outside and explain that they are going to work together to "build" the Earth. First have each of the kids pick a part to play by drawing a slip from the hat. Then, using the information provided, explain what each "part" does. Let the kids practice any sounds or movements and then build the Earth from the inside out. Here's how:

1. Have the child playing the part of the *inner core* flex his or her muscles (or pretend to lift weights) and stand in the center of the area. Tell the kids that this represents that the inner core is very dense and is solid metal.

2. Next have the *outer core* kids form a circle around the inner core. They should face in, toward the inner core. Then have them walk counterclockwise around the inner core while holding their arms out to the sides and waving them up and down. Tell the kids this represents the fact that the outer core is liquid and is moving.

3. Have the children playing the *deep mantle* join hands to form a circle around the outer core. (Have them chant, "hot rock, hot rock, hot rock.")

4. Have the *asthenosphere* kids surround the deep mantle. (Have them slowly sway their bodies back and forth to represent the movement that occurs in this layer.)

5. Finally, have the *lithosphere* kids form a circle around the *entire rest of the Earth.* Have them face outward and *slowly* walk around the rest of the Earth. (Have them chant, "moving plates, moving plates.")

(continued next page)

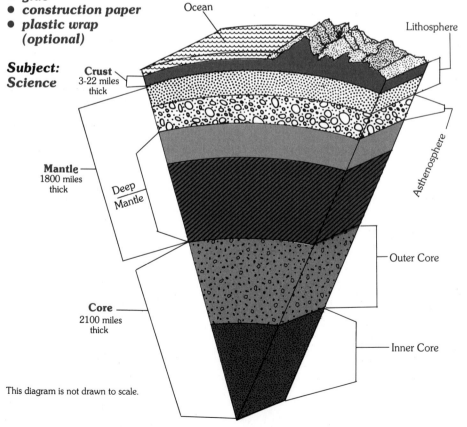

Ocean

Lithosphere

Crust
3-22 miles thick

Asthenosphere

Mantle
1800 miles thick

Deep Mantle

Outer Core

Core
2100 miles thick

Inner Core

This diagram is not drawn to scale.

Luise Woelflein

A MODEL EARTH

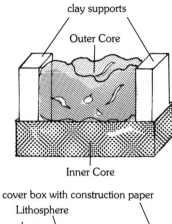

clay supports

Outer Core

Inner Core

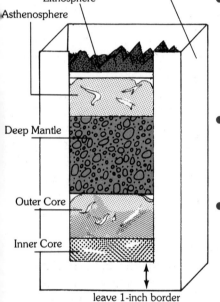

cover box with construction paper

Lithosphere

Asthenosphere

Deep Mantle

Outer Core

Inner Core

leave 1-inch border

After the kids have made a "living" Earth, have them work in groups to make cross-sections of the Earth's layers. First divide the kids into groups of six and give each group a fairly tall, thin cardboard box (two-pound baking soda boxes, large raisin boxes, and confectioner's sugar boxes work well) and other supplies. Have each group make a model by following the directions below. (Encourage the kids in each group to divide up the work. For example, one person could be responsible for making one layer and another could decorate the box. When everyone's layer is finished, they can assemble their models from inner core to lithosphere.)

- **The Box**—Cut off the box top and save it for the lithosphere. Then cut out a panel from one of the sides of the box. *Do not* cut off an entire side—leave about a one-inch (2.5-cm) border around the edges (see diagram). Cover the box with construction paper.
- **Inner Core**—Cut out several pieces of cardboard so that they fit inside the bottom of the box. Glue the pieces in a stack and let dry. Cover the stack with construction paper.
- **Outer Core**—Fill a small Ziplock bag (sandwich bags work well) with approximately one inch (2.5 cm) of water. Get all the air out and then seal the bag. Use masking tape to tape over the seal and the top of the bag so the bag stays closed. To keep the upper layers of the model from putting too much pressure

on the bag, make two clay supports as shown. (In time, water *will* leak from the bag. If you want to use the models for a long-term display, have the kids replace the water with crumpled plastic wrap.)
- **Deep Mantle**—Make a block of deep mantle out of dough (see end of activity for recipe). It should fit inside the box and be about three inches (7.5 cm) thick. Let it dry and then paint it with watercolors or poster paints.
- **Asthenosphere**—Add red food coloring to a handful of dough and mix well. Put the dyed dough into a small Ziplock bag to keep it soft. Get all of the air out, and seal the bag. Use masking tape to reinforce the seal. Mash the dough in the bag so that it will fit into the box.
- **Lithosphere**—Trim the box top so it fits inside the walls of the box. This piece of cardboard will separate the upper mantle from the crust. To make the upper mantle part of the lithosphere, cover the bottom of the cardboard box top with a thin, flat layer of dough. Next make the crust by covering the top of the cardboard with a thin layer of dough and adding extra dough for mountains and hills. Let dry and then paint both parts.

Note: The layers of the Earth are not believed to be as distinct as is represented in these models. Between all of the Earth's layers there are transition zones and each layer varies in thickness and density. Many geologists disagree on exactly how the layers interact with each other to produce changes on the Earth's surface.

HOW TO MAKE THE DOUGH

Two batches of this recipe will make enough dough for five models.

- **4 cups baking soda**
- **2 cups cornstarch**
- **2½ cups cold water**

Mix all of the ingredients in a medium-sized saucepan and cook over medium heat, stirring constantly. Cook about 10 minutes or so, until the mixture is the consistency of mashed potatoes. Remove from heat, turn out onto a plate, and then cover with a damp cloth. After the dough cools, knead it gently into a smooth ball. Then store it in a tightly sealed plastic bag and refrigerate until you're ready to use it.

Plates on the Go

Plot earthquakes on a world map, and then talk about plate movements.

Objectives:
Describe how earthquakes are related to plate tectonics. Plot earthquake data on a world map using longitude and latitude. Describe several geological events that can happen when two plates meet.

Ages:
Advanced

Materials:
- *world map showing latitude and longitude*
- *map pins or straight pins with colored heads*
- *copy of earthquake data provided in the activity*
- *copies of the questions on page 12*
- *copies of page 16*
- *pencils or pens*
- *paper*

Subjects:
Science and Geography

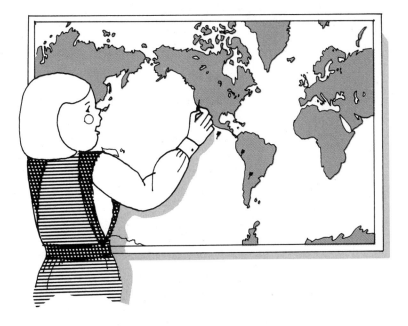

Every year nearly a million earthquakes occur in the world. But of these only a few thousand are strong enough to be felt by people and fewer than 50 may do a lot of damage. By plotting earthquakes on a world map the kids in your group will learn more about where earthquakes occur and why they happen.

Before you get started, make copies of the earthquake data and the questions on page 12. (Remember not to copy the answers.) Then hang a world map on a bulletin board where everyone can see it. (Be sure the map has latitude and longitude marked on it.)

Begin the activity by asking the kids what they know about earthquakes. How long do they last? Can earthquakes happen anywhere? Are they more likely to happen in one place than another? You can use the information on pages 5 and 8 to discuss what they know, but don't explain too much at this point. You just want to be sure that everyone understands what an earthquake is, how long earthquakes normally last, what the magnitude of an earthquake is, and how scientists measure an earthquake's magnitude.

Then tell the kids that they are going to plot some earthquakes on a world map. The earthquakes are actual earthquakes of magnitude 6.1 or greater that occurred during 1983, 1984, and 1985.

Divide the data that you copied earlier among the kids, giving each child some earthquakes to plot. You might want to review latitude and longitude with the kids so that they know how to find the correct points on the map. Then pass out map pins and give the kids some time to plot the quakes.

When the kids are finished ask them if they see any pattern as to where the quakes have occurred. (After plotting the points, the kids should be able to see that most of the earthquakes occurred along plate boundaries in the Pacific Ocean.) Do they have any ideas why this happened? Tell them that almost all earthquakes are caused by the movement of rock along fractures in the Earth, called *faults*. Then explain that the Earth's surface (the crust plus the top portion of the mantle) is believed to be divided into several large plates that slowly move. As the plates move, they pull apart, collide, or slide past each other. This movement creates the stress that forces rocks to break along faults.

Pass out copies of page 16 and explain that the map shows where the plate boundaries are believed to be. Have the kids compare these maps with the one they used to plot the earthquakes. Explain that all the plate boundaries did not show up on the map they used to plot the earthquakes because they plotted only a few of the earthquakes that happened during 1983-1985. If they could plot more earthquakes, especially ones of lower magnitude, they could get a better idea of each plate's boundaries—but it would take plotting thousands of earthquakes!

Point out the arrows on page 16 and explain that they represent the direction each plate is moving. Then, using the information on pages 4-5, explain what happens along plate boundaries when plates move apart from each other, smash together, or slide past each other.

Finally, pass out copies of the questions you copied earlier. After the kids have finished, go over the answers (see page 12). *(continued next page)*

PLATE PUZZLERS

1. Is the Atlantic Ocean getting bigger or smaller? (bigger)
2. Name a plate that does not carry a continent or part of a continent. (Cocos, Nazca, Philippine, and Scotia Plates [*Note:* The Pacific Plate carries a small piece of North America.])
3. Where on the seafloor would you expect to find older rock—near the middle of the Atlantic Ocean or close to the coast of North America? (near the coast)
4. Why is the island country of Iceland growing wider each year? (It straddles the Mid-Atlantic Ridge, so as the plates pull apart magma oozes to the surface and creates more land.)
5. What geologic features might you ex-pect to find along the west coast of South America? (Because there is a subduction zone along the west coast of South America, you would expect to find mountains and volcanoes in this area.)
6. Based on the plate movements shown on your Copycat Page and what you know about plate tectonics, how would you explain the existence of the Himalaya Mountains? (The Indo-Australian plate is moving northward and is slowly shoving India into Eurasia. As these two continents collide their crust is buckling up into mountains. [You might want to point out India on the map so the kids can get a better picture of this.])

EARTHQUAKE DATA

DATE	LATITUDE	LONGITUDE	MAGNITUDE	DATE	LATITUDE	LONGITUDE	MAGNITUDE
1-13-92	1N	127E	6.0	7-12-93	42N	139E	6.0
2-13-92	15S	166E	6.1	8-7-93	26N	125E	6.0
3-2-92	52N	159E	6.5	8-8-93	12N	144E	7.1
3-4-92	3S	147E	6.0	8-20-93	5S	142E	6.0
3-5-92	52N	159E	6.3	9-6-93	4S	153E	6.2
4-25-92	40N	124W	6.3	9-18-93	36N	71E	6.1
5-17-92	7N	126E	6.4	9-22-93	6S	154E	6.1
5-12-92	16S	172W	6.4	9-29-93	18N	76E	6.3
5-21-92	41N	88E	6.5	10-13-93	5S	146E	6.4
5-25-92	19N	77W	6.3	10-24-93	16N	98W	6.3
5-27-92	11S	165E	6.5	11-11-93	50N	177W	6.3
6-25-92	28S	176W	6.1	11-13-93	51N	158E	6.5
6-28-92	34N	116W	6.3	12-9-93	0	125E	6.5
7-10-92	44N	149E	6.2	12-20-93	6S	131E	6.4
7-13-92	3S	76W	6.1	1-10-94	13S	69W	6.4
8-2-92	7S	121E	6.9	1-17-94	34N	118W	6.4
8-4-92	12S	166E	6.1	1-21-94	1N	127E	6.2
8-7-92	57N	142W	6.3	2-11-94	18S	169E	6.4
8-19-92	50N	174W	6.2	2-12-94	20S	128W	6.3
8-19-92	42N	73E	6.6	2-12-94	20S	169E	6.4
8-28-92	0	13W	6.3	3-9-94	18S	178W	6.6
9-11-92	6S	26E	6.7	3-14-94	1S	23W	6.2
9-15-92	14S	167E	6.3	4-18-94	6S	154E	6.6
9-30-92	51N	178W	6.1	4-27-94	21S	173W	6.2
10-11-92	19S	168E	6.4	5-2-94	1S	97E	6.2
10-18-92	7N	76W	6.6	5-24-94	23S	122E	6.2
10-23-92	42N	45E	6.1	5-31-94	7N	72W	6.3
11-4-92	14S	167E	6.1	6-6-94	2N	76W	6.4
12-12-92	8S	121E	6.5	6-9-94	13S	67W	7.0
12-18-92	6S	147E	6.0	6-18-94	42S	171E	6.2
12-20-92	6S	130E	6.6	7-13-94	16S	167E	6.4
1-10-93	59S	26W	6.3	7-13-94	7S	127E	6.5
1-15-93	43N	143E	6.9	7-21-94	42N	132E	6.5
1-20-93	7S	128E	6.2	7-25-94	56S	27W	6.3
2-7-93	37N	137E	6.3	8-4-94	6S	131E	6.2
3-1-93	3S	138E	6.1	8-14-94	44N	150E	6.2
3-6-93	10S	164E	6.1	8-19-94	26S	63W	6.4
3-20-93	56S	97W	6.0	8-30-94	44N	150E	6.2
3-21-93	18S	178W	6.1	9-1-94	40N	125W	6.6
4-5-93	59S	26W	6.0	9-16-94	22N	118E	6.5
4-18-93	11S	76W	6.0	10-4-94	43N	147E	7.3
5-2-93	56S	24W	6.3	10-5-94	43N	147E	6.2
5-13-93	55N	160W	6.4	10-8-94	1S	127E	6.4
5-24-93	22S	66W	6.6	10-9-94	43N	147E	6.5
5-30-93	1N	127E	6.0	10-16-94	45N	149E	6.4
6-8-93	51N	157E	6.4	11-5-94	57S	157E	6.1
6-8-93	31S	69W	6.5	11-15-94	5S	110E	6.2
6-18-93	29S	176W	6.2	12-10-94	18N	101W	6.6
7-11-93	25S	70W	6.2	12-28-94	40N	143E	6.4

Data courtesy of the U.S. Geological Survey, Golden, Colorado.

Mauna Kea, a Hawaiian volcano, is the tallest volcano in the world. When measured from its base on the ocean floor to its summit, it is over 33,000 feet high—more than 4400 feet higher than Mt. Everest!

In the winter of 1811-1812, a series of earthquakes in New Madrid, Missouri, set off geysers, caused islands to disappear from the Mississippi River, and rattled windows in Washington, DC.

During a severe earthquake in Alaska in 1964, huge cracks appeared on the Earth's surface. Some of these cracks were three feet wide!

In 1906 plates on either side of the San Andreas Fault shifted 20 feet and caused a huge earthquake in San Francisco.

Old Faithful, a geyser in Yellowstone National Park, can shoot a column of water over 180 feet into the air.

Krakatoa was a volcanic island in the South Pacific. Its eruption in 1883 was marked by four explosions—the loudest of which was heard 3000 miles away! Krakatoa's eruption set off a tsunami that was about 100 feet tall.

When Mount St. Helens erupted on May 18, 1980, it sent a cloud of ash 12 miles into the air.

Tsunamis can sweep through the ocean at 600 miles per hour. That's faster than the cruising speed of a jet plane!

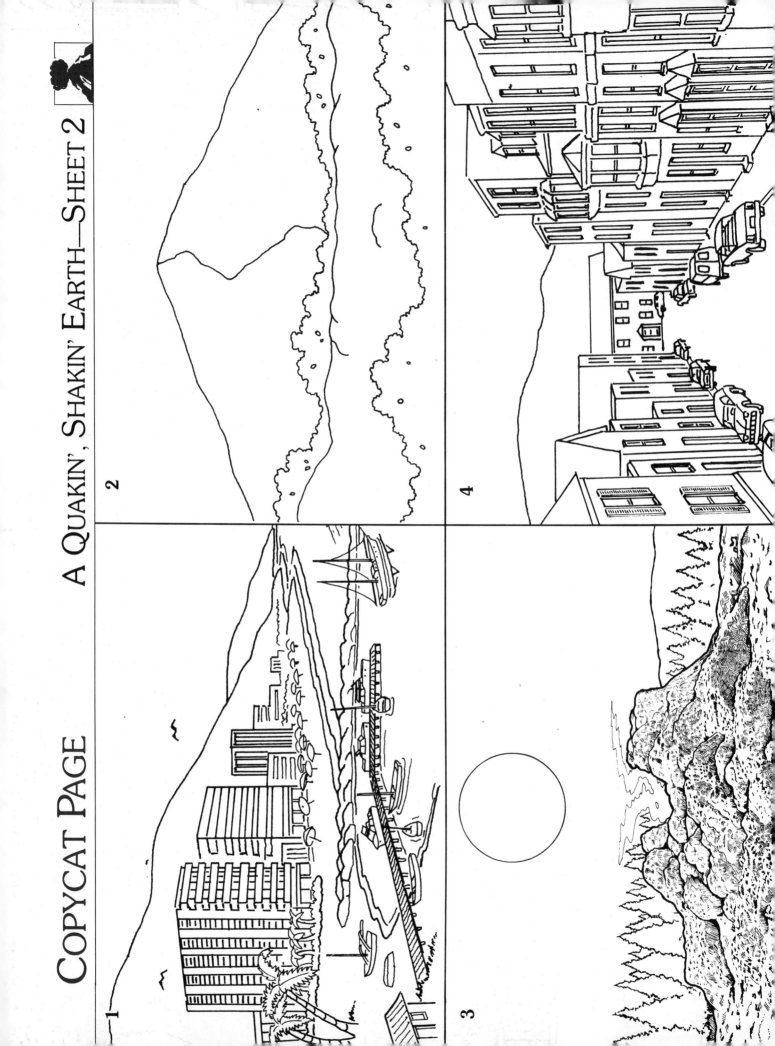

1

2

3

4

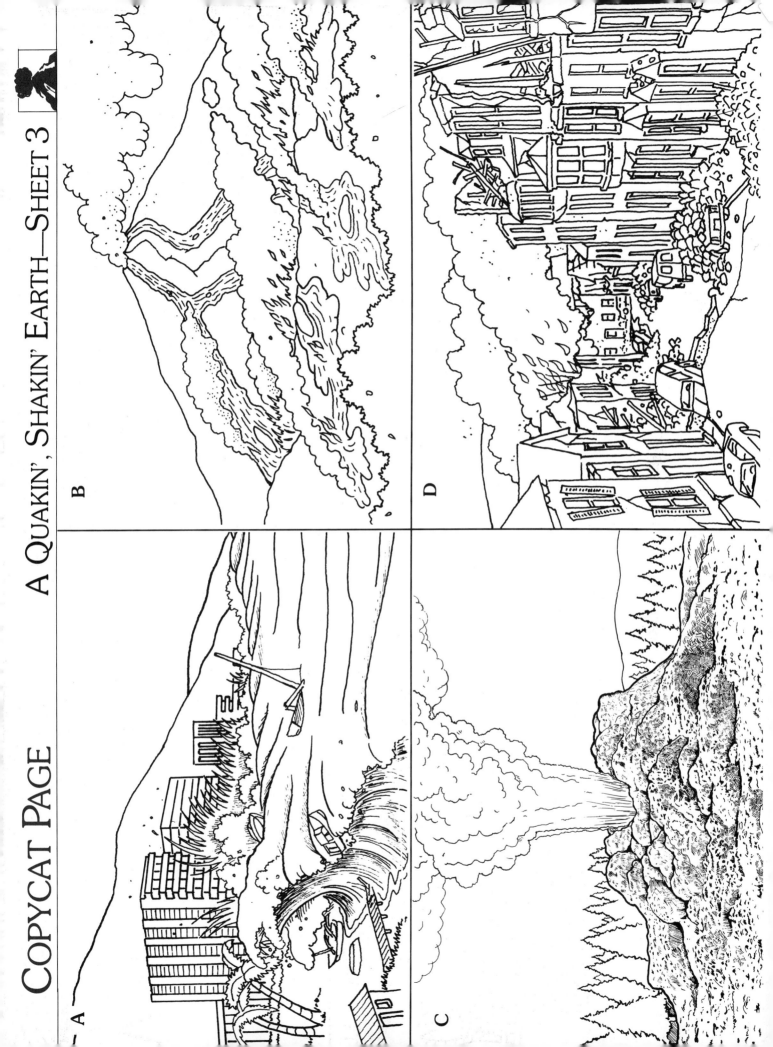

A

B

C

D

COPYCAT PAGE

PLATES ON THE GO

▲▲▲ plates colliding   ——— plates moving apart   ------- plate boundary not well known

Note: This is a simplified map of plate boundaries. We have marked only a few of the many places where plates are sliding past each other. (These areas are marked with this symbol: ★)

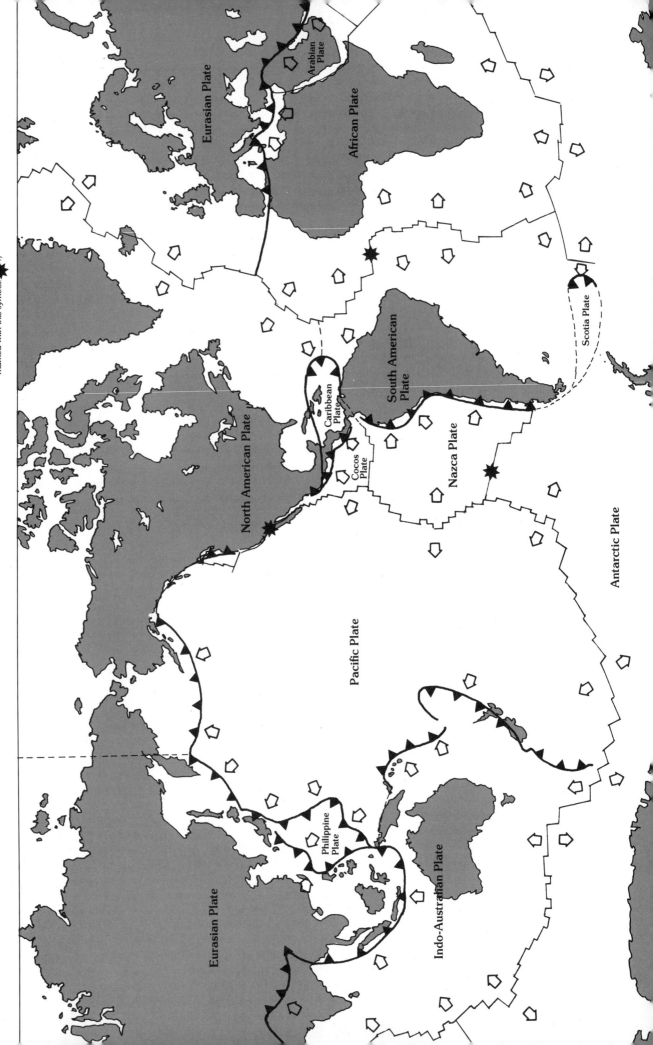

Eurasian Plate

Arabian Plate

African Plate

North American Plate

Caribbean Plate

Cocos Plate

South American Plate

Nazca Plate

Scotia Plate

Pacific Plate

Antarctic Plate

Philippine Plate

Eurasian Plate

Indo-Australian Plate

ROCKS AND MINERALS

Millions of years ago, on the southern tip of what is now Africa, a pocket of molten rock deep within the mantle started to rise. As the magma forced its way up, it carried pieces of rock that had formed in the mantle, including bits of crystallized carbon.

Millions of years later, children hiking along a river found a piece of the crystallized carbon lying on the ground and began playing with it. The bit of carbon looked like a shiny pebble of clear, hard glass. It turned out that these children had been playing with a diamond—one of the most valuable minerals in the world. And their discovery led to the famous South African diamond rush of the late 1800s.

Diamonds are just one example of the thousands of minerals that can be found in the Earth. Although not all minerals happen to be as brilliant, hard, and rare as diamonds, all provide clues about the make-up of the Earth. And minerals form rocks—the building blocks of the planet.

WHAT MAKES A MINERAL A MINERAL?

In the days of Aristotle, people thought minerals possessed supernatural powers and had living spirits within them. Pliny the Elder thought that some minerals were made of magic substances that formed in the stomachs of animals and could kindle fires, quiet the wind, increase intelligence, and protect the unborn.

We've come a long way from Pliny in understanding what minerals are and how they form. For example, we know that all minerals are made up of one or more chemical elements. (Elements are substances that cannot be broken down chemically into other, simpler substances. An example is oxygen.) But elements also make up corn, cats, trees, and everything else on Earth. So what makes a mineral different from other substances?

The Make-Up of Minerals: Although not all geologists agree on the exact definition of a mineral, most do agree that a substance must fit these four general criteria to be called a mineral:

- **Lifeless Lumps**—Minerals are inorganic, which means they do not form from the remains of plants, animals, or other living things. Some minerals form as magma cools or as a liquid solution evaporates. Others form as one mineral changes into another, such as when graphite changes to diamond with increasing pressure.

- **Naturally Occurring Stuff**—Minerals are solid substances that occur naturally in the Earth. Although scientists have learned how to make some minerals, such as diamonds, most geologists use the term "mineral" to mean a naturally occurring substance.

- **The Same, Through and Through**—Minerals have the same chemical make-up wherever they are found. For example, the mineral quartz always consists of one part silicon (an element) to two parts oxygen (another element). Some minerals, such as gold, copper, and sulphur, are made up of just that element. But most minerals are combinations of several different elements. (So far, scientists have identified 92 elements that occur naturally in the Earth's crust. Most of these, such as oxygen and silicon, usually occur only in combination with other elements. But 22 of the elements, including gold, carbon, silver, and sulphur, can occur freely.)

(continued next page)

- **Repeating Patterns**—The atoms that make up the elements of a mineral are bonded together in specific repeating patterns. This orderly arrangement of atoms is what forms a mineral's characteristic crystal shape. For example, a crystal of salt, which is made up of the elements sodium and chlorine, is always cube-shaped because the two kinds of atoms are "stacked" alternately in a boxlike form. But sometimes, depending on how a mineral grows, the symmetrical pattern on the inside does not show up on the outside. For example, if salt does not have much room to grow, it will not form characteristic crystal shapes on the outside, even though the atoms inside are still arranged in the same orderly fashion.

The size of a crystal depends on how long it was growing and how much space was available. For example, minerals that form when magma cools quickly are usually tiny. But if magma cools slowly, large mineral crystals can form. And some of the largest crystals form when minerals crystallize slowly from a solution. (See "Grow a Crystal" on page 26 for more about crystals and how to grow them.)

Sorting Out: It's easy to tell the difference between a piece of rose quartz and a hunk of turquoise. Rose quartz is a pale pink and turquoise is a bright sky blue. But it's not quite as easy to tell a piece of quartz from a piece of calcite. Even though these two minerals have completely different chemical make-ups, they often look very similar to an untrained eye. And it's not just different minerals that are hard to tell apart. Even the same mineral can look very different, depending on where and how it formed. For example, quartz can be pink, clear, milky, blue, or lavender, depending on whether traces of iron, nickel, or other chemical impurities are present.

Because many minerals have similar characteristics and the same type of mineral can vary in appearance, geologists consider many different characteristics in order to identify minerals. Besides comparing color, they also look at the way the surface of a mineral reflects light (luster); check to see whether a mineral splits in a special way (cleavage); and determine the crystal shape, hardness, specific gravity, magnetic properties, and whether or not a mineral glows under an ultraviolet light. (See "Mystery Minerals" on page 25 for more about how to identify minerals.)

Geologists have discovered over 2000 different kinds of minerals, but only about 10-20 of these make up about 90 percent of the Earth's crust.

Million Dollar Minerals: We walk on quartz, mica, calcite, and other minerals every day and usually don't think twice about it. But when someone flashes a brilliant red ruby or a fiery opal our way, we take notice. Minerals that are unusually beautiful and are also rare and durable are called *gemstones,* or precious minerals. Most gemstones are colorful crystals of common minerals. For example, sapphires and rubies are varieties of the mineral corundum. And emeralds are a variety of the mineral beryl. (For more about how gemstones are used, see "Beyond Beauty" on page 59.)

WHAT MAKES A ROCK A ROCK?

Most people think all rocks are rigid. But a type of rock called itacolumite, found in parts of India and North Carolina, is easy to bend with your hands. Most people also think all rocks are heavy. But if you drop a huge piece of pumice into water, it will float. So what is a rock? Geologists define rocks as substances that are made up of one or more minerals. For example, granite is a rock made up of the minerals

quartz, mica, feldspar, and sometimes hornblende. And basalt is a rock made up of the minerals plagioclase and pyroxene. Most rocks are made up of several major minerals, as well as a few minor ones. But some rocks are made up of mainly one type of mineral. For example, limestone is made mainly of the mineral calcite.

Rocks are the building blocks of the Earth. They make up the crust, the mantle, and the core. But unlike minerals, rocks are not the same through and through. For example, granite does not always contain the same proportions of quartz, mica, feldspar, and hornblende. In addition, the size of the mineral crystals may vary. And because of this, different granites can look different and have different physical properties.

One of the Family: The Earth's crust is made up of dozens of different types of rocks, but each forms in one of these three ways:

- **Born to Flow:** *Igneous rocks* form when magma cools and hardens. Some igneous rocks form underground when magma that is pushed up toward the crust cools and crystallizes before it reaches the surface. Granite, gabbro, and dolerite are three kinds of igneous rocks that form underground. But other igneous rocks such as basalt and obsidian form on the Earth's surface when lava cools and hardens.

- **The Layered Look:** *Sedimentary rocks* are layered rocks. Most get their start as wind, ice, and water wear down rocks into bits of sand, soil, mud, pebbles, clay, and other loose sediment. As this sediment washes into rivers, lakes, and oceans, it piles up, layer upon layer. Over time, as the pressure on the bottom layers increases, the sediment compacts and cements together to form solid rock. For example, sandstone is a sedimentary rock that is made up of layers of compressed and cemented sand grains (usually quartz). And shale is a sedimentary rock made up of layers of mud (very fine-grained quartz, feldspar, and clay minerals).

  Sometimes sedimentary rocks form by the evaporation of water that contains various substances dissolved in it. When the water evaporates, the minerals crystallize. Two examples of sedimentary rocks that form in this way are halite (formed from dissolved sodium chloride) and some types of limestone (formed from dissolved calcium carbonate).

  Coal, chalk, and a few other sedimentary rocks form from organic material, such as the shells, skeletons, and other parts of plants and animals. For example, shellfish can remove calcite dissolved in the water they live in and use it to build their shells. When these animals die, their shells pile up on the bottom and limestone often forms as the shells become cemented together.

- **The Pressure's On:** When igneous and sedimentary rocks are subjected to intense heat and pressure deep within the Earth, their mineral composition and grain size can change, and they become *metamorphic rocks*. For example, metamorphism can recrystallize the calcite grains in limestone into a larger size, forming marble. And shale, when subjected to intense heat and pressure, changes into the metamorphic rock called slate. You can often see new minerals in metamorphic rock, such as garnets, as well as once-flat sedimentary layers that have been bent and twisted from the heat and pressure.

Change Is the Game, Rock Is the Name: Wind, water, and ice are continually wearing away igneous, metamorphic, and sedimentary rocks and creating new sedimentary rocks. (See pages 31-33 for more about how wind, water, and ice shape the landscape.) And with each volcanic eruption and plate subduction, new rocks are always "in the works." By studying rocks and how they "recycle," scientists can learn more about how the Earth itself is changing, and how life has changed over time.

Discover Rocks!

Collect some rocks, make a graph, and make a paper mosaic of granite.

Objectives:
Observe, describe, and sort different rocks. Explain that rocks are made of minerals.

Ages:
Primary

Materials:
- *samples of granite*
- *hand lenses (optional)*
- *chalkboard or easel paper*
- *copies of page 29*
- *strips of pink, yellow, and black construction paper*
- *scissors*
- *glue*

Subjects:
Science, Art, and Math

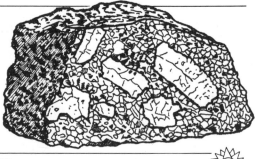

What are rocks made of? Do all rocks look the same? In this activity, your group can find out the answers to these and other "rocky" questions by taking a close-up look at granite and several other types of rocks.

PART 1: SEARCH, SORT, AND GRAPH

First take your group on a rock hunt outside so the kids can search for their own special rock samples. (See "Rock Hounding Tips" on page 22 for suggestions about where to look.) Have them try to find four or five interesting and different-looking rocks to bring inside to study.

Once you're back inside, have the kids sit in a circle. Tell them to study each of their rocks carefully. (You can pass out hand lenses to let them get a closer look.) Explain that they should think about how each rock looks and feels.

Then have each child pick out a favorite rock and put the others aside for the time being. Have them think up words that describe their rocks. Then go around the circle, making a list of these words on a chalkboard or piece of easel paper. If the kids have trouble thinking up adjectives, you can suggest some, such as sparkly, jagged, or rough.

Now have the children get into small groups and put *all* their collected rocks in a pile. Tell each group to separate their rocks into two piles according to any of the characteristics they just came up with. For example, the kids could sort their combined collections into piles of rocks that are dark or light, smooth or rough, shiny or dull, and so on. Let them come up with some other ways to sort the rocks, such as by color, size, or shape.

Now have your kids make a simple graph to illustrate some of their rock characteristics. First have each person retrieve his or her favorite rock from the group piles. While they're doing this, draw a graph on a chalkboard or large piece of easel paper and number the vertical axis, as shown, including enough marks for the number of children in your group. Then use the words the kids thought up to describe their favorite rocks and list them along the horizontal axis.

For each word, ask how many have a rock that fits that description. Then choose a child to come up and show on the graph how far the line should go. (You can make either a line or bar graph.)

When the graph is completed (see diagram), explain to the group that you now have information about all their rocks in a picture called a graph. Ask questions about their rocks and have them use the graph to figure out the answers. Try some simple math problems too. For example, if there are 15 kids in your group and 3 of them have rocks that are shiny, how many have rocks that are dull?

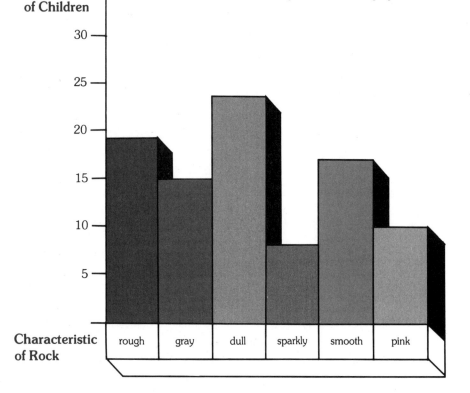

Number of Children

30
25
20
15
10
5

Characteristic of Rock: rough, gray, dull, sparkly, smooth, pink

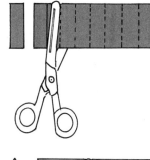

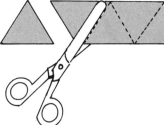

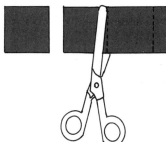

PART 2: MINERAL MOSAICS

Now explain that rocks are made up of *minerals*. (For more about rocks and minerals, see the background information on pages 17-19.) Tell the kids that scientists who study rocks can often classify a rock by identifying the minerals that are in it. For example, the minerals feldspar, quartz, and mica or hornblende make up a rock called *granite*.

Pass around some samples of granite. (You can get samples of granite and other minerals at some museums or rock and mineral shops. Also see "Where to Get Rock and Mineral Samples" on page 69 in the bibliography for addresses of some science supply companies.) If the kids look closely, they will be able to see the different minerals. (You might want to have them use a hand lens to get a clearer

Sample Mosaic

picture.) Most of what they see in granite is probably feldspar, which looks gray, white, or pink. The clear, glassy mineral is quartz. And the dark speckles are mica or hornblende. (Mica is a very shiny mineral; hornblende appears dull.)

Tell the kids that they will "make" their own piece of granite using bits of colored paper. Though everyone's rock will have the same "minerals," none of the "rocks" will look exactly alike. Explain that this is also what happens in nature. Granite is always made up of the same minerals, but the amount of each mineral varies from rock to rock. Here's how to make a rock mosaic:

First pass out copies of page 29, which shows a stylized drawing of a piece of granite. Also give each child one strip each of pink, yellow, and black construction paper. Have them cut small pieces of each color as follows: pink rectangles for feldspar, yellow triangles for quartz, and black squares for mica or hornblende (see diagram). Then have them glue the pieces in a mosaic pattern on the area enlarged by the hand lens (see diagram). Also have them glue one of each shape in the appropriate box on the page.

After all the "rocks" are finished, display the results and compare the different patterns.

Be a Rock Hound!

Collect rocks and put them on display.

Objective:
Describe how to start a rock collection.

Ages:
Primary, Intermediate, and Advanced

Materials (all optional):
● *rock and mineral field guides*
● *backpacks or collecting bags*
● *first aid kit*
(continued next page)

Having your kids start their own collections is probably the best way to get them excited about rocks and minerals. And no matter where the kids search—right near your school or nature center or at another site—they'll be sure to find some good "collectibles." (Local chambers of commerce, libraries, nature centers, natural history museums, and college and university departments of geology should all have information about good rock and mineral collection sites to visit in your area.)

Before you set out on your search, you

might want to have the kids look at some examples of the kinds of rocks they might find. Contact a local college or university geology department, nature center, or museum to see if they have a collection your group can look through. You might also want to have them read one or more of the following articles from *Ranger Rick*:
● "Strike It Rich" (September 1985)
● "When You Find a Rock" (May 1978)
● "You Can Be a Rock Hound" (July 1986)

Next go over the following tips with the kids. Then pack up your field guides and other gear and give rock hounding a try!

(continued next page)

- *masking tape*
- *pencils*
- *notebooks*
- *newspaper*
- *geologists' hammers and picks*
- *safety goggles*
- *hand lenses*
- *glue*
- *shallow boxes*
- *shoe boxes or egg cartons*

**Subject:
Science**

ROCK HOUNDING TIPS

Where to Look: Rocks show up just about anywhere, but some spots are better collection sites than others. If you can, have your group look in mountainous country, volcanic regions, and along outcrops (areas of exposed bedrock). Beaches, river banks, and stream beds can also be good places to "hound." And road cuts and cliff bases can be real collecting hot spots too.

Quarries, mines, and construction sites are often good places to look for rocks, but they can be dangerous.

What to Bring: Depending on how serious you want to get with your rock hounding, you can have the kids use a lot of equipment—or almost none at all. You might want to have the kids simply pick up any rocks they find and make a display out of them. (You can even have them start their collections with "store-bought" specimens. Many rock and mineral shops and museums sell samples of different kinds of rocks. You can also order rocks from certain catalogs. See "Where to Get Rock and Mineral Samples" on page 69 in the bibliography.) But hardcore hounders will need safety goggles, hand lenses, masking tape, pencils, field guides, notebooks, backpacks, and geologists' hammers or picks. (Hammers and picks are often available at army surplus, hardware, and geology supply stores. But make sure you get hammers and picks that are made especially for rock hounding. Regular hammers and picks may crack or shatter when used to break off rock samples.)

Drawing by Pidgeon

How to Hound: You don't have to follow a set procedure when rock hounding, but here are some simple steps you might want to have your kids follow:
- Pick up or hammer off a small rock specimen (one that fits comfortably in your hand).

- Mark a number on a piece of tape and stick it on the rock. Write the number and a brief description of the rock in a notebook. Also write in the date and the place where you found the rock.
- Wrap the rock in some newspaper for protection before putting it in your backpack or collecting bag.

Preparing Your Collection: After returning from your hounding hike, have the kids wash the dirt from their rocks so they can get a good look at them. (It's also easier to see colors when a rock is wet.) Another way to get a good idea of a rock's true features is to wrap it in cloth or newspaper and break it open with a hammer. (The inside isn't worn and weathered like the outside.) The kids can use a hand lens to look for signs of fossils, crystals, flecks of metal, and so on.

You can have the kids sort their rocks any number of ways. For example, they could categorize them according to color, how they formed (igneous, metamorphic, or sedimentary), kind (limestone, granite, shale, and so on), or the area in which you found them. After the kids sort their collections, they can make simple display cases for them by gluing the rocks inside a shallow box. Or they can store the rocks in a shoe box or egg carton. Either way, tell the kids to be sure each rock is labeled so they'll have a record of their collections.

Code of Common Sense and Courtesy: Here are a few guidelines that rock hounds should always keep in mind:
- Take only what you need for your collection.
- Never go rock hounding by yourself. And always let someone know where you're going and when you plan to return.
- Wear boots or sturdy shoes.
- Take along a snack and something to drink. A first aid kit is a good idea too.
- Always ask permission before hounding on private land, in quarries, or in parks. (Keep in mind that many parks don't allow collecting of any kind. It's always a good idea to ask first.)
- When climbing on loose rock, make sure nobody is below you.
- Stay out of caves and mine shafts.
- Stick to trails when you can, especially in parks and on private property.
- Carry out your litter when you leave.
- *Always* wear safety goggles when chipping at rocks. And make sure people close to you have goggles on too.

Carla Calcite

Listen to a story about Carla Calcite and the changes she goes through and then make a Carla Calcite storybook.

Objective:
Describe several ways that rocks change over time.

Ages:
Intermediate

Materials:
- *story on page 24*
- *copies of page 30*
- *blank 5 × 8" index cards (7 per child)*
- *scissors*
- *tape*
- *glue*
- *crayons or markers*
- *pens or pencils*
- *samples of shale, slate, phyllite, schist, and gneiss (Optional—see "Where to Get Rock and Mineral Samples" on page 69 in the bibliography.)*
- *heavy paper (optional)*

Subjects:
Science and Language Arts

Most people probably don't think of rocks as objects that change much. But some rocks go through a lot of changes during their "lifetime." Here's a way to help your kids understand some of these changes.

First talk a little about the three main types of rocks (igneous, sedimentary, metamorphic) and the processes that form them. (See the background information on pages 18-19.) You might want to bring in some samples of shale, slate, phyllite, schist, and gneiss to explain how certain rocks can change into other types of rocks. Using the rock samples, you can explain that shale (a type of sedimentary rock) forms when clay minerals are compacted together. If the shale is subjected to heat and pressure, it can become the metamorphic rock called slate. And if it's subjected to progressively greater heat and pressure, it can metamorphose into phyllite, then into schist, and finally into gneiss.

Next explain that most rocks are made up of several different kinds of *minerals*. (See the background information on pages 17-18.) Some, though, are made up of only one mineral. For example, in its purest form, marble is composed mainly of the mineral called calcite.

After your discussion, pass out copies of page 30 and have the kids cut the pictures apart. Tell them that they will be listening to a story about the adventures of Carla Calcite, a small bit of calcite. (Note: The story and the pictures on page 30 represent a very simplified account of how rocks can change. For example, limestone can form in a variety of ways, and limestone can change into marble under a variety of conditions.) By listening to the story, your kids will be able to see that rocks can change over time. The pictures on the Copycat Page illustrate some of Carla's adventures. As the kids listen to the story, they should try to arrange the pictures in the correct sequence.

When you've finished reading the story, go over the pictures and their correct order and have the kids number each one. (See the answers at the end of the activity.) As you talk about which part of the story each picture represents, explain that these kinds of changes happen very, very slowly. Millions of years often pass between one stage and the next.

Now pass out seven index cards to each person and have the kids follow the directions given below to make their own Carla Calcite storybooks.

HOW TO MAKE A STORYBOOK

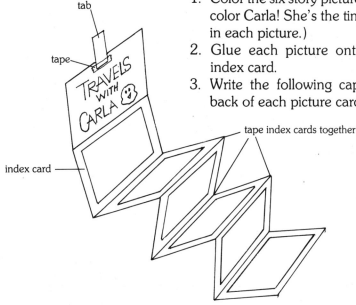

1. Color the six story pictures. (Be sure to color Carla! She's the tiny smiling face in each picture.)
2. Glue each picture onto a separate index card.
3. Write the following captions on the back of each picture card:

Picture 1—Carla falls to the bottom of the sea.

Picture 2—All the layers are pressed and cemented together. Carla is now part of a sedimentary rock called limestone.

Picture 3—Continents move together. Carla's rock changes into a metamorphic rock called marble. Carla is pushed up into a mountain.

Picture 4—People cut blocks of marble out of the hillside. Carla's block is loaded onto a cart.

Picture 5—A sculptor carves a statue out of the marble Carla is in.

Picture 6—The Minerva statue is very old. Pieces of marble have broken off. Carla will eventually erode away.

(continued next page)

4. Put the six cards in order and tape them together along the edges on both sides (see diagram on page 23).
5. To make the book's cover, tape the seventh card above Picture 1 and write the title of the story on it.

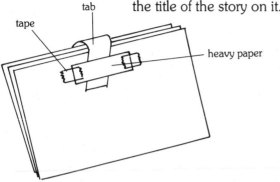

6. Fold the booklet, accordion-style.
7. To make a closure for your storybook, cut a ½ × 3-inch (1.3 × 8-cm) strip of index card or heavy paper. Fold the strip in half and tape or glue the ends of it to the top center of the title card so that you have a tab about 1½ inches (4 cm) long. Cut another strip about ½ × 1½ inches (1.3 × 3.8 cm) and tape its ends across the bottom center of the back of the last picture card. Slip the tab through the strip to close the storybook.

Answers: 1—C; 2—B; 3—F; 4—A; 5—D; 6—E

THE ADVENTURES OF CARLA CALCITE

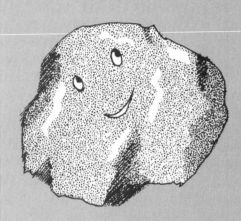

In the boot-shaped country of Italy stands what's left of a marble statue of Minerva, the Roman goddess of wisdom. Down near Minerva's foot, in the fold of her robe, is a small bit of mineral called Carla Calcite.

Carla wasn't always a part of the marble statue. In fact, she's been through a lot of changes in her lifetime. Where did she come from? And how did she end up in a marble statue? To find out, we'll have to travel back many millions of years—to a time when the world looked very different from the way it looks today.

If you went to northern Italy right now, you'd see a group of mountains called the Alps. But long ago in that very same spot, there were no mountains at all. There wasn't even an Italy. Instead, there was a great sea. Carla was around then, but she was not part of a rock statue. She was part of a shell.

The shell Carla Calcite was part of was the shell of a tiny creature that had lived in the great sea. When the animal died, its shell settled on the bottom of the sea together with the shells of many, many other sea animals. The shell—and Carla—then sat on the seafloor for thousands of years. As they sat there, layers of other shells, along with other sediment, slowly piled on top of them.

All those layers were very heavy, and the weight packed and squeezed Carla and other bits of minerals together. Chemicals in the seawater seeped into the tiny spaces around Carla and the other bits of minerals, cementing them together. All of this pressing and cementing hardened the layer of shells Carla was in until it finally turned into a kind of rock called limestone. Millions of years passed by, and the layers kept right on piling up.

During this time the whole Earth was changing—just as it always has. The pieces of land that were north and south of the great sea were slowly moving toward each other like huge rafts. The movement crumpled the old sea bed Carla was in until all the rock layers in it—including Carla's layer—were folded together like an accordion.

All of this folding caused mountains to form where the sea had once been. The heat and pressure from forces inside the Earth gradually changed Carla's limestone layer into a new kind of rock. Now Carla was part of a layer of rock called marble. And after many millions of years, Carla's marble layer was pushed up until it was near the top of a huge hill.

One day, there was the *chink, chink* sound of sharp tools chipping away at the hillside. All of a sudden, a huge block of marble fell away from the hill. A group of men tugged and heaved as they hoisted the block up onto a cart. Carla was inside this block, and she was about to start a new journey.

The cart carried Carla and her block to a little town where a sculptor lived. He bought the block, and soon began to chip away at it with his stone-cutting tools. As he sculpted, the shape of the goddess Minerva gradually took form. And that's how Carla came to be in the fold at the bottom of the robe near the foot of the marble statue.

But our story of Carla doesn't necessarily end there. For over a thousand years, the sun beat down on Minerva and so did the rain. The rainwater dissolved small bits of the statue. And bit by bit, tiny pieces of rock fell away from Minerva and were washed into a river.

One day Carla may wash into the river too. And eventually she may fall to the river bottom, becoming covered with layers of silt and rocks. The layers may slowly become cemented together. And it may only be a matter of time before Carla finds herself inside a layer of rock once more.

Mystery Minerals

Identify several minerals by examining some of their properties.

Objectives:
Investigate some of the properties of minerals. Identify several common minerals.

Ages:
Intermediate and Advanced

Materials:
- *samples of quartz, graphite, pyrite, hematite, galena, and halite (See "Where to Get Rock and Mineral Samples" on page 69 in the bibliography.)*
- *6 streak plates (available at some rock and mineral shops) or pieces of porcelain tile, each with an unglazed side*
- *6 pennies*
- *6 pairs of steel scissors or 6 steel files*
- *6 index cards*
- *chalkboard or easel paper*

Subject:
Science

With about 2000 minerals in the world, how do geologists tell one from another? They look at certain mineral properties: color, hardness, luster, and so on. This activity will help your kids learn how to use some of these properties to identify six common minerals.

Before you begin, set up six different stations around the room. Equip each station with a numbered index card (i.e., "Station #1," "Station #2," and so on), a streak plate, a penny, a pair of steel scissors or a steel file, and a mineral sample. Then make an enlargement of the blank chart shown on page 26 and pass out a copy to each person.

To start off the activity, explain to the kids that geologists can tell which minerals are which by looking at certain mineral characteristics, or *properties*. Then tell the kids that they'll be trying to identify some common minerals using some of the same properties geologists use. (You should point out that geologists also use many other tests in addition to the ones here and they also use much more sophisticated equipment.)

To help the kids get started, run through the properties of one of the minerals. For example, hold up the piece of quartz so that *everyone* can see it, but don't tell them which mineral it is. Explain that one property that helps geologists identify a mineral is its color. Have the kids write the color of quartz in the first row of the "color" column on their charts. (Quartz is usually colorless or white, but it may be pink, smoky gray, yellow, or purple if it contains impurities.)

Now test the *streak,* or the color a mineral leaves behind when scratched across a streak plate or piece of unglazed porcelain. (Quartz should leave a white streak.) Point out that many minerals leave a streak that's a different color from the mineral itself. (Also tell the kids that it's sometimes difficult to distinguish the streak of very hard minerals.) Have the kids fill in the correct box on their charts, then move on to the "luster test."

Luster is the way a mineral reflects light. Slowly move the quartz around so that it catches the light. Quartz and many other minerals have what's called a *glassy* luster because they shine like glass. Certain other minerals reflect very little light and have what's known as a *dull* luster. And still others have a *metallic* luster: They shine brightly, just as a piece of gold or silver would. (*Note:* The luster of some minerals can vary. For example, graphite and hematite can be dull or metallic, depending on the samples you have.)

Once the kids have filled in the luster box, lead them through the test for the mineral's hardness. (For the purposes of this activity, we are using a very simplified hardness test.) Explain that if you can scratch a mineral with your fingernail, it's rated as being *very soft.* If you can scratch it with a penny but not your fingernail, it's considered to be *soft.* If you can scratch it with a pair of steel scissors or a steel file but not a penny, it's *medium.* And if the scissors or file won't make a scratch in the mineral, it's *hard.* The steel probably can't scratch the quartz, so quartz is considered to be a hard mineral. Have the kids fill in the box for hardness.

Note: Tell the kids that many of their test results will vary, depending on the quality of the mineral samples they used and how each person interpreted the results of each test.

Now have the kids work in pairs to determine the properties of the five remaining mystery minerals. They should go from station to station, filling in each box on their charts, except the minerals' names. (Since each group will be starting at a different station, remind the kids to match each station number with the appropriate row on their charts.) When the kids are finished, copy the mineral key shown on page 26 onto the chalkboard or a piece of easel paper, making sure you don't list the minerals in the same order as the stations are set up in. (If you use minerals other than the ones we've suggested, use a rock and mineral field guide [see the bibliography] to verify their streak, luster, and other properties.) Then have the kids use the information to identify all six of the minerals they've worked with. Also tell the kids that although there are thousands of minerals, only a few dozen make up over 90 percent of the minerals found in the Earth's crust. Here's some information you can use to talk about each mineral as you go over the answers:

WHICH MINERAL IS WHICH?

QUARTZ
Quartz is a common mineral found in many kinds of rocks. It is used to make glass, as well as many other products. When it contains certain impurities, it can form gemstones such as amethyst.

GRAPHITE
The word *graphite* comes from the Greek word meaning "to write." This mineral, which is used to make the writing point in pencils, is often mistakenly called "lead." Graphite is often used as a lubricant too.

HALITE
Halite's Greek name means "salt." It's the same substance we use to flavor our food.

HEMATITE
Hematite is the most important source of iron. It's also a source of red pigment.

GALENA
Galena is a major source of lead. It often forms cube-shaped crystals.

PYRITE
Pyrite is commonly known as "fool's gold" because its crystals are gold-colored. It often occurs near its more valuable look-alike.

MINERAL KEY

COLOR	STREAK	LUSTER	HARDNESS	NAME
gray	dark gray	metallic	soft to medium	galena
colorless (may have tints of color)	white	glassy	soft	halite
colorless, white (may have tints of color)	white	glassy	hard	quartz
brassy yellow, gold	blackish	metallic	hard	pyrite
gray	gray, black	dull, metallic	very soft	graphite
red, brown, gray, black	dark red, reddish-brown	dull, metallic	hard	hematite

SAMPLE CHART

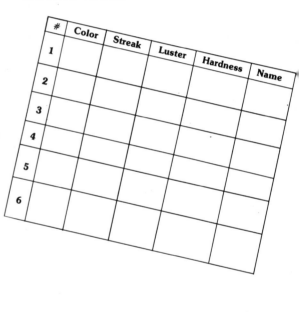

Grow a Crystal

Grow crystals from a chemical solution.

Objectives:
Define crystal. Describe how crystals grow. Explain that minerals are composed of crystals.

Ages:
Intermediate and Advanced

ugar, snowflakes, and most other non-living substances, including most of the Earth's minerals, may occur as crystals. In this activity your kids will be able to learn more about crystals by growing their own crystals from a chemical solution.

Before starting the activity, talk about what crystals are and how they are formed. (See the background information on pages 17-18 and "Facts About Crystals" on page 28.) Also show the kids pictures and samples of some common minerals that have characteristic crystal shapes, such as quartz and halite.

Now follow the directions on the next page for growing crystals. (For younger children, you may want to grow one crystal yourself as a demonstration. Older kids may work individually, in pairs, or in small groups to grow their own crystals.)

Materials:
- saucepan
- heat source (such as a stove or heating coil)
- glass jars
- saucer or shallow dish
- spoon
- water
- thread
- pencils
- hand lenses (optional)
- samples of minerals (See "Where to Get Rock and Mineral Samples" on page 69 in the bibliography.)
- pictures of crystals
- alum (obtained from a pharmacist or chemist)
- baby food jars
- plastic wrap
- ice water
- large containers
- small buttons

Subject:
Science

1. Put some water in a saucepan and stir in some alum (about two ounces [56 g] for each cup [240 ml] of water you use).

2. Heat the solution but don't let it boil.

3. Remove the pan from the heat and stir in more alum until no more will dissolve. This will give you a *saturated* solution. (You'll know your solution is saturated when you see a few particles of alum starting to settle out on the bottom.)

4. Pour a little of the alum solution into a saucer or shallow dish. Place the dish in a draft-free place where it will remain undisturbed. Then pour the remainder of the solution into a clean jar and cover it for later use.

5. As the solution in the dish cools and some of the water evaporates, small crystals will begin to form. After a few days, these "seed" crystals should be big enough to handle (about ⅛-¼ inch [3-6 mm] across). Tie one end of a piece of thread around one of the seed crystals and tie the other end around a pencil.

6. Pour the solution from the covered jar into a clean jar, leaving behind any crystals that may have formed. Then

suspend the seed crystal completely in the solution by placing the pencil across the top of the jar (see diagram). Leave the crystal undisturbed so it can continue to grow.

Older kids should observe, monitor, and record the development of their crystals. Have them use these questions as a guideline for record-keeping:

- What chemical compound did you use?
- When did you mix the chemical solution? (time and date)
- When did you first notice crystals appearing?
- When did you suspend the seed crystal in the solution?
- What color is your crystal?
- How many *faces* (smooth, flat surfaces) does your crystal have?
- What does your crystal look like? Draw a picture of it.

Remind the children that they should not handle the crystal while it is growing because this might add impurities and affect the way the crystal grows. (See "Crystal-Growing Tips" on the next page.) After the crystals stop growing, the kids can remove them from the solution, dry them off, and compare them.

(continued next page)

Luise Woelflein

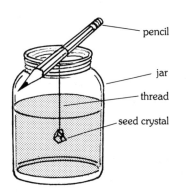

pencil

jar

thread

seed crystal

CRYSTAL-GROWING TIPS

- Although alum is a safe compound, it should be used carefully. After working with the solution, always wash hands and containers thoroughly.
- The temperature of the water determines how much of the alum will dissolve (hot water holds more chemical in solution than cold water). A solution that is saturated at a high temperature becomes supersaturated as it cools, causing the alum to fall out of solution and form a crystal. As water evaporates, the same thing happens.

- To grow a crystal with smooth, distinct faces, allow it to grow with as little interference as possible. Don't let it touch other crystals or the sides or bottom of the jar.
- To grow a single, large crystal, "persuade" the alum to collect only onto one seed crystal. Periodically remove any other crystals that form in the jar. And cover the solution with cloth or a paper towel to allow slow evaporation while keeping out dust. (Bits of dust in the solution give new crystals places to start growing.)

FACTS ABOUT CRYSTALS

- Minerals form when their chemical components combine together in specific combinations. They can crystallize from a vapor, a solution, or magma. (Most of the Earth's natural crystals in rocks grow from magma.)
- The atoms that make up minerals are bonded together in specific repeating patterns, and it's this orderly, repeating arrangement of atoms that forms the characteristic crystal shapes we see.
- Crystals begin to form as evaporation occurs or as temperature or pressure drops.
- If cooling or evaporation is slow, large crystals have time to grow. Tiny crystals will form if cooling or evaporation is speeded up.

- Although crystals represent the symmetrical pattern of their internal structure, many factors (such as temperature, pressure, rate of evaporation, amount of space available, type of solution, and so on) can affect their growth.
- Because crystal-growing conditions can vary, crystals of the same chemical make-up may develop into different sizes and shapes. But despite the variations in form, the angles between the crystals' faces will always be the same.
- Because crystals seldom can grow in an unconfined space without touching other growing crystals, large, perfectly formed crystals in nature are rare.

#1 Ice water

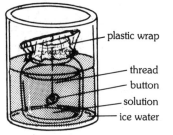

- plastic wrap
- thread
- button
- solution
- ice water

#2 Room temperature

#3 Hot water

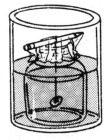

BRANCHING OUT: SET UP AN EXPERIMENT

The kids can test their scientific thinking by conducting a crystal-growing experiment. Here's how:

1. Mix one part alum to two parts water. Heat and stir the solution until the alum dissolves.
2. Loop a piece of thread through a button and tie the ends of the thread around a pencil. (The button will act as a "seed" for the crystals to grow on.) Do the same with two other buttons.
3. Pour equal amounts of solution into three baby food jars. Suspend a button in each jar of solution, then cover the jars with plastic wrap.
4. Set one jar of solution in a container of ice water. Set another jar in a container of water that's just been boiled. Set the last jar in a container of room temperature water as a control.

5. Have the children hypothesize what will happen in each jar. Will crystals grow more quickly in one jar than in the others? Will crystals grow larger in one of the jars? Have the kids give reasons for their answers.
6. Have the kids observe what happens in each jar, checking about every 15 minutes for several hours. (Although the results might vary, the smallest crystals should form in the "cold water" container. And these crystals should begin to form right away. The largest crystals should form in the "hot water" container, but they should grow much more slowly. The size of the crystals and rate of crystal formation should be intermediate in the control jar.) Then explain that results can vary greatly with crystal-growing experiments because it's easy for the containers or solutions to get contaminated. For example, if one of the jars was dirty, it might have affected how the crystals grew.

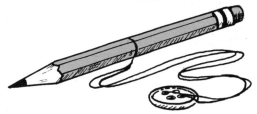

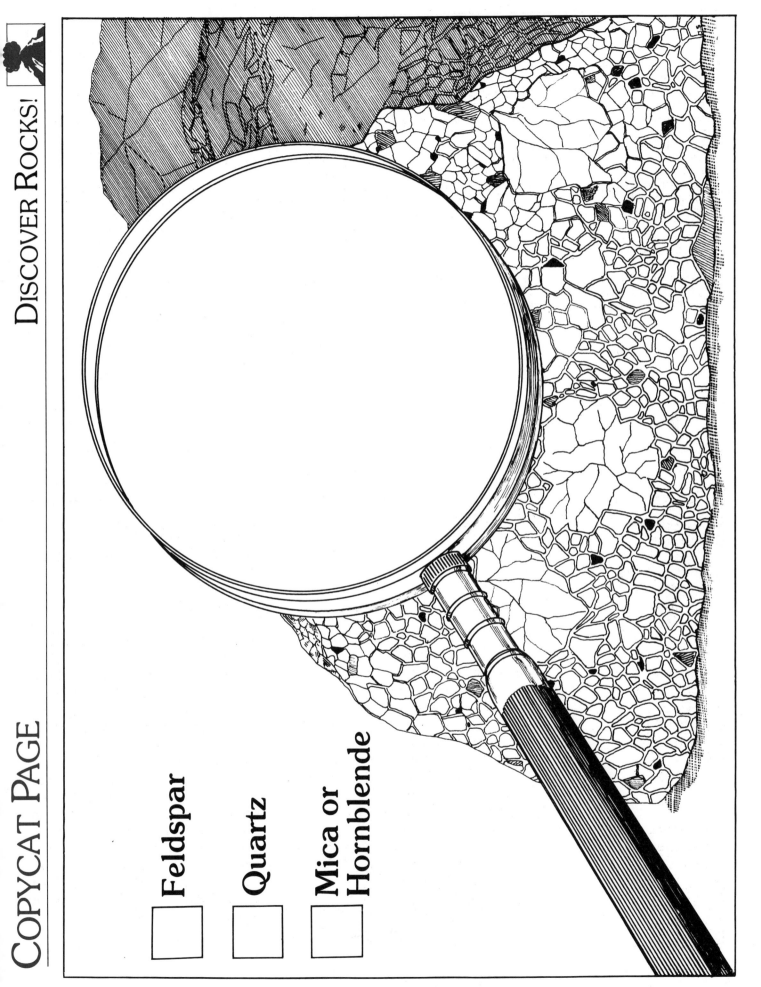

COPYCAT PAGE

Feldspar

Quartz

Mica or
Hornblende

COPYCAT PAGE

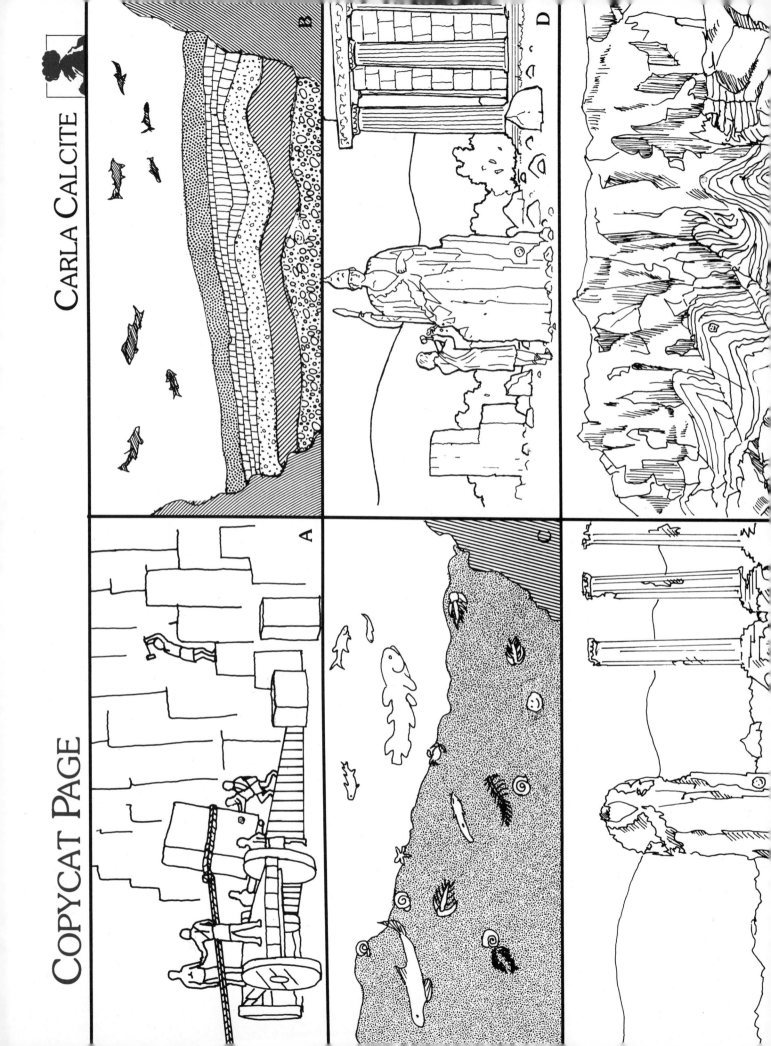

SHAPING
THE LANDSCAPE

T he Indians called it *Unka-timpe-Wa-Wince-Pock-ich,* or "the red rocks standing like men in a bowl-shaped canyon." Ebenezer Bryce, the first settler to arrive there, thought it was "a dandy place to lose a cow." Today this spot in Utah is known as Bryce Canyon, and many people consider it to be one of the wildest and most beautiful canyons in the world, with bizarre rock towers, deeply cut gorges, and flat-topped mesas.

The beauty of Bryce Canyon is mainly due to the work of fast-flowing water, blowing sand, chemical reactions, and freezing temperatures. These geologic "agents" have been eating away at the rocks that make up the canyon for millions of years. And geologists estimate that in another million years or so even its more resistant rock towers will have crumbled.

All of the Earth's landforms, from mountains to caves to coastlines, are subjected to many of the same "wear and tear agents" that are working away at Bryce Canyon. But at the same time that landforms are slowly being worn away, new ones are constantly being built. In this chapter, we'll look at how landforms are continually created and destroyed.

THE "WEAR-IT-DOWN" FORCES

Two forces—weathering and erosion—are constantly at work wearing away the rocks that make up the Earth's crust. *Weathering* causes rocks to fragment, crack, crumble, or break down chemically. *Erosion* loosens and carries away the rock debris caused by weathering. Over time these two forces, working together, can change the shape of the land.

As Rocks Crumble: Weathering

All rocks weather, but not in the same way or at the same rate. It all depends on the mineral composition of a rock, as well as where the rock is located. Here's a closer look at the ways rocks weather:

- *The Freeze and Crack Cycle:* When water seeps into cracks in rocks and freezes, it can force a rock to split. That's because when water freezes it increases in volume. And because it needs more room, it pushes against the rock, eventually causing it to break apart. This is called *ice wedging.* If freezing and thawing occur over and over again, "solid" rocks can eventually be reduced to rubble.

- *The Roots of Destruction:* Plants do their share of breaking up rocks. For example, plants can grow in the small bits of soil that collect in the rock cracks that form from ice or chemical action. As the plant's roots grow, they expand and apply pressure to the rock, forcing the crack to widen and deepen. Eventually, roots can split apart rocks—even large boulders and pieces of bedrock.

- *The Chemical Breakdown:* Some minerals are changed into different minerals as they react with chemicals in air and water. But not all minerals react in the same way. For example, when iron is exposed to the oxygen in the Earth's atmosphere, it changes chemically into iron oxide, or rust. Other minerals, such as pyrite, form weak acids when they dissolve in rainwater, and these acids help to decompose the rocks. *(continued next page)*

The Stuff of Soil: There's a big plus to weathering—a plus we couldn't live without. As rocks are continually broken down into smaller and smaller bits, they eventually get so small the particles become fine enough to be called silt or sand, two important ingredients of soil. Although soil is mostly made up of tiny rock fragments, it also contains decayed plant and animal material (called humus), such as rotten leaves and decomposed animal bodies. This rich material provides the nutrients that plants need to grow.

Water, Wind, and Ice on the Move: Erosion

Raindrops falling on a field in Iowa, a glacier scraping out a valley in the Alps, and the wind whipping across the face of the Great Sphinx in Egypt are all examples of erosion at work. Erosion continues the work that weathering starts by helping to loosen particles and by transporting weathered rock material. The main agent of erosion is running water. It probably does more to wear away the land than all the other geologic agents combined. But ice and wind are also important landscape sculptors.

Eroder #1: Water

Water, Water, Everywhere: A fast-flowing stream carries a lot more than water. Soil, sand, silt, pebbles, and even boulders are sometimes carried along with the current. And as these rocks and pieces of rock get carried along, they carve out a variety of different landforms, from stream valleys to mesas.

Underground H_2O: Some of the precipitation that falls on the surface of the Earth eventually seeps into the ground and becomes *groundwater*. Groundwater can remove underground limestone bedrock by dissolving it and slowly carrying it away. Very weak acids in the water "eat away" at these rocks, often producing underground caverns. Some caverns get so big their ceilings collapse, forming depressions on the Earth's surface called *sinkholes*.

Coast Carvers: Moving water also shapes the coastlines of the continents. As powerful waves carrying rocks and sand pound against the land, they can cause extensive erosion, which can form rugged cliffs, arches, and coastal caves.

Eroder #2: Wind

Sand in the Face: Wind by itself isn't much of an erosion agent. But high-speed wind carrying a load of dust and sand is. Wind erosion is responsible for shaping a variety of landscape features, especially in desert areas. (Deserts usually have few plants to hold the soil in place with their roots.) Wind erodes by lifting and removing sediment, but it can pick up only very fine, dry particles, sand size and smaller. Wind carrying sand can also sandblast rock and is responsible for many of the towers, pinnacles, and polished bedrock in desert landscapes.

Eroder #3: Ice

A Slice of Ice: In a few places, the climate is so cold that most precipitation falls as snow. In these areas, more snow accumulates than melts each year. As the snow piles up hundreds of feet thick, it presses down on the bottom layers until the snowflakes are pressed tightly together. Over time they become interlocking ice crystals and form a huge sheet of solid ice called a *glacier*.

Eventually, the solid mass of ice starts to "flow" slowly downhill. This motion, usually just a few inches per day, is due to two processes. First, the layers of ice that make up a glacier start to slide over one another. Second, the ice at the very bottom of the glacier, where the pressure is highest, starts to melt. The thin layer of water that forms beneath the glacier allows the block of ice to slide very slowly over rocks and soil.

We are currently experiencing an *interglaciation*, a period between the most recent deglaciation and the beginning of the next glaciation, or glacier age. The present interglaciation is different because, for the first time in the Earth's history, humans are changing the environment. Scientists believe another glacier age lies ahead. But, because of human interference—especially the intensification of the atmosphere's greenhouse effect, often called *global warming*—they cannot predict when or how it will occur.

Giant Ice Scrapers: As a glacier travels, it plucks out chunks of bedrock, which become embedded in the ice. These fragments of rock help grind and gouge the land as the glacier keeps moving. Glaciers scrape out a variety of landforms, from steep peaks, such as the famous Matterhorn in the Alps, to U-shaped valleys and narrow ridges.

Ice Ages Gone By: Glaciers from past ice ages have shaped many of the landscape features we see today, including many of our northern lakes, hills, and valleys. The last Ice Age ended about 10,000 years ago as the ice sheets that covered the northern part of North America, Europe, and Asia slowly melted. As the ice sheets retreated, they left canyons, huge boulders (called "erratics" because they are out of place), scratched rock surfaces, piles of rocky debris, and other evidence that glaciers had once covered the land. The melting of ice sheets also caused the sea level to rise and re-cover the continental shelves adjacent to the continents.

THE "BUILD-IT-UP" FORCES

As weathering and erosion wear away the Earth's crust, other forces are constantly at work building it up. Most of the building—especially the "big stuff"—is the result of plate tectonics. Mountains, volcanoes, and faults are formed as rocks are pushed up, warped, folded, or fractured. (For more about plate tectonics, see pages 4-5.) But smaller-scale building can also be done by the same agents—water, ice, and wind—that tear the Earth's crust down. These three agents carry the sediment produced by weathering and erosion and dump it somewhere else. The build-up, or *deposition,* of this sediment creates new landforms. And just like weathering and erosion, deposition is an ongoing process.

Move It and Dump It: Most of the sediment from weathering and erosion is carried and dumped by flowing water. And most of it eventually ends up in an ocean. For example, every day, the Mississippi River dumps over two million tons (1.8 t) of sediment into the Gulf of Mexico. But some of the sediment carried by wind, water, and ice ends up in other places too, such as at the bases of mountains (forming alluvial fans), along river and stream banks (forming flood plains), and at the retreating edges of glaciers (forming huge piles of rock, rounded hills, and other landscape features). Deposition also forms dunes, beaches, and other landforms.

The Layered Landscape: Over the years, sediment from oceans, rivers, and streams piles up, forming layers of sedimentary rock as the sediment is compressed. Geologists can study sedimentary layers to find out more about the ancient environment and life that lived in an area. For example, if sedimentary rock layers are not turned upside-down by the shifting of the Earth's crust, geologists know that the oldest fossils will be found in the lowest rock layers and the youngest fossils will be found in layers closer to the Earth's surface. (For more about fossils, see pages 42-44.)

PEOPLE SHAPE THE LANDSCAPE

So many forces are at work on the Earth's crust at the same time that it's often hard to figure out which geologic agents are responsible for what you see. But many landscape features aren't caused by geologic forces at all. They're caused by people. We speed up erosion by clearing land for farming, housing developments, lumbering, and strip mining; we change the courses of rivers by building dams and channels; and we cut through mountains of rock to build highways. All of these changes, as well as other human activities, affect the natural patterns of erosion, weathering, and deposition.

Mountain Blocks

Discuss some mountain facts and then make a mountain picture cube.

Objectives:
Describe what mountains are made of, how they change over time, and where they are located. Explain how mountains affect people and wildlife.

Ages:
Primary and Intermediate

Materials:
- *pictures of the Himalaya, Rocky, and Appalachian Mountains*
- *copies of page 40*
- *crayons or markers*
- *glue*
- *scissors*
- *tape*
- *map of the world*
- *manila folders or heavy construction paper*

Subject:
Science

ajestic. Snow-capped. Mysterious. Massive. All of these adjectives describe mountains—the tallest landforms on Earth. Mountains cover about one-fifth of the world's total land area and they exist on every continent, including Antarctica. Introduce your group to these diverse landforms and then have them make a mountain picture cube to review what you discuss.

First have the kids sit in a circle as you show them pictures of mountains and ask them some mountain-related questions. (Choose the questions that fit the level of your group.)

- What are all mountains made of? (rock)
- How do mountains differ? (Show them pictures of the Himalayas, the Rockies, and the Appalachians. Explain that some mountains are very steep, with jagged cliffs and high peaks, while others look more like low, tree-covered hills.)
- What's the difference between a mountain and a mountain range? (Explain that sometimes a mountain, such as a large volcano, may stand alone. But most mountains form clusters, with many grouped very close together. These mountains form a mountain range.)
- Do mountain ranges exist underwater? (Yes. Some of the longest mountain ranges in the world are underneath the oceans. And some of the peaks in these ranges, which are usually volcanic peaks, stick up through the surface, forming islands.)
- What is the highest continental mountain in the world? (Mt. Everest, in Tibet and Nepal. It is 29,028 feet [8708 m] high.) What is the highest oceanic mountain in the world? (Mauna Kea, on the island of Hawaii. It rises 33,476 feet [10,043 m] off the ocean floor.)
- How does the temperature change when you climb a mountain? (It gets colder as you get higher. And that's one of the reasons different kinds of plants

and animals live in different places on a mountain.)
- How does the temperature affect the types of plants that grow on a mountain? (Near the bottom of a mountain, where the air is warmer, there are many plants and some of them are very tall. As you get higher and the temperature gets colder, there are fewer plants and most are short and stubby. And at the very top of a high mountain, it is too cold for most plants, including trees, to grow. On high mountains, you'll find either bare rock or rock covered with ice and snow.)
- Can you name some animals that live on mountains? (mountain sheep, mountain goats, giant pandas, pikas, mountain quail, snow leopards, and so on; explain that some of these animals are especially adapted to mountain life)
- Where do mountains exist today? (Point out major mountain ranges on a map of the world.)
- What are some ways people use mountains? (for hiking, skiing, mountain-climbing, farming [coffee], mining ores and other minerals, and so on; the beauty of mountains also inspires art, music, poetry, and photography)
- Do mountains ever change? (Yes, all mountains are constantly changing. They wear away from the action of wind, water, and ice, and they rise as plates collide.)
- Can you explain what a glacier is? (Explain that some mountains are so high that the snow that falls on them does not melt and sometimes packs together to form huge sheets of moving ice called glaciers. Glaciers move very slowly—usually only a few inches a day—but they can carve deep valleys, scratch rock surfaces, and shape mountain peaks.)
- How do mountains form? (All mountains form as a result of changes deep inside the Earth. For example, volcanoes form when melted rock from inside the Earth erupts and piles up.

Other types of mountains form when huge pieces of the lithosphere, called plates, interact with each other. For more about plate movements, see pages 4-5.)

After talking about mountain landforms, pass out a copy of page 40 to each person. Have the kids color in the pictures and then follow these directions to make a mountain picture cube to review what

you've discussed.

1. Glue page 40 to a manila folder or heavy piece of construction paper and let it dry.
2. Cut along the outer solid lines.
3. Fold along the solid inner lines to make a cube. To make the folding easier, you might want to show the kids how to score the fold.
4. Tape the faces of the cube together.

The Contour Connection

Take a look at a topographic map and then use it to make a model of the landscape it portrays.

Objectives:
Describe what a topographic map is. Explain what contour lines show.

Ages:
Intermediate and Advanced

Materials:
- *copies of page 41*
- *cardboard*
- *scissors*
- *pencils*
- *clay*
- *reference books*
- *map of the world*
- *paper*
- *markers or crayons*
- *thumbtacks*
- *yarn*

Subjects:
Science and Geography

Contour Map #1 should look something like this.

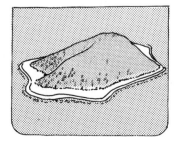

I t takes a special map to really show the landscape. And topographic maps *are* special. In this activity your group will learn more about "topo" maps by taking a look at one and creating models of what it shows.

Begin by passing out copies of page 41. Give the kids a chance to look at the map, then ask them to describe the area shown. Also ask them if they know what the solid, curved lines and the numbers represent. Explain that the lines are called *contour lines*. On this map the contour lines show

how high above sea level the land is. (There are also maps with contour lines depicting areas, such as the seafloor, that are *below* sea level.) Each contour line on page 41 represents a change in elevation of 20 feet (6 m). The number associated with each contour line represents the elevation of the Earth's surface where the line passes through. Explain to the kids that it's possible to show depressions on contour maps by putting hachure marks

Hachure marks show depressions.

Contour Map #1

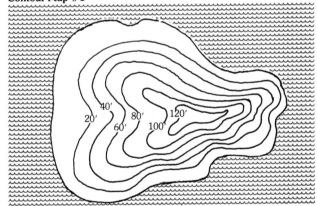

along them (see diagram below).

Tell the kids that the map on page 41 is an example of a *topographic*, or *contour*, map. Together, all of the contour lines on such a map represent the shape or contour of the land area that the map portrays.

Ask the kids if they can tell from the lines where the ground is gently sloping and where it is steep. (Where the distance between the contour lines is great, such as on the right-hand side of the map, the land is not very steep. However, where the contour lines are close together, such as

on either side of the stream near the top of the map, the ground rises very quickly and the slope is steep.) Now tell the kids that they are going to turn the map into a three-dimensional model so that they can really see what the contour lines are showing.

Pass out several pieces of cardboard, a pencil, scissors, an extra copy of page 41, and a lump of clay to each child. Then have them follow these directions to make

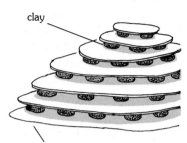

clay

cardboard contour pieces

their models. (You might want to have the kids work in pairs.)

1. Trim off the borders at the top and bottom of one of the maps. Then cut the map apart *along the 120' contour lines only.* You should end up with two pieces that have contour lines marked on them plus a third piece with the stream on it. Set the stream piece aside. (You'll be using it later.)

2. Lay one of the large pieces you have cut out onto the cardboard and trace its outline. Label it 120'. Then reduce the size of the piece by cutting along the 140' contour line.

3. Trace this new, smaller piece onto a different part of the cardboard and label it 140'. Then continue cutting along contour lines representing progressively higher elevations. Each time

trace the new, smaller piece and label each one.

4. Repeat steps 2 and 3 with the other section of your original map.

5. Cut out each of the cardboard tracings. You should end up with 12 pieces.

6. Using your second contour map as a guide, stack the pieces from lowest to highest elevation. (You will be making two stacks of cardboard.) As you stack the layers, stick several small balls of clay between each pair. (This will help make the model a little higher so you can see more easily what the contours show.)

7. Lay the stream piece between the two stacks.

When they are finished making their 3-D models, the kids should be able to see the "canyon" that the stream runs through. Explain that a skilled topographic map reader can look at a map like the one the kids worked with and instantly imagine what the landscape of the area looks like. As a follow-up to the activity, pass out copies of the small contour maps shown on pages 35 and 36 and let the kids draw what they think the areas actually look like. (Contour Map #1 on page 35 shows an island, and Contour Map #2 on this page shows a volcano.)

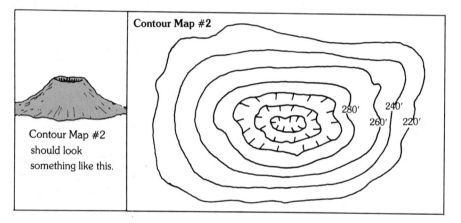

Contour Map #2

Contour Map #2 should look something like this.

280' 240'
260' 220'

BRANCHING OUT: TAKE A LOOK AT LANDFORMS

LANDFORMS IN THE UNITED STATES:
Adirondack Mountains
Appalachian Mountains
Black Hills
Bryce Canyon
Cape Cod
Devil's Tower
Grand Canyon
Great Plains
Mammoth Cave
Mauna Loa
Mississippi Delta
Mount St. Helens
Niagara Falls
Rocky Mountains
San Andreas Fault

LANDFORMS AROUND THE WORLD:
Alps or the Matterhorn in Europe
Andes Mountains in South America
Ayers Rock in Australia
Azores in the North Atlantic Ocean
Giant's Causeway in Northern Ireland
Highlands in northern Scotland
Himalayas or Mount Everest in Asia
Hsi Chiang River Delta in China
Iceland in the Atlantic Ocean
Island of Surtsey in the North Atlantic
Lake Baikal in the Soviet Union
Marianas Trench in the Pacific Ocean
Mount Etna in Italy
Mount Fuji in Japan
Mount Kilimanjaro in Tanzania
Mount Vesuvius in Italy
Pyrenees Mountains in Spain and France
Rift Valley in Africa
Rock of Gibraltar off the coast of Spain
Southerland Falls in New Zealand
Victoria Falls in South Africa
White Cliffs of Dover in England

Here's a way for your kids to learn about some of the world's diverse landforms. Copy each of the landforms listed here on a separate slip of paper and have everyone choose one. Tell each person to research his or her landform and write a short paragraph about what it is, how it formed, and why it is unique. Then have each person draw a picture to illustrate the information. It can be a picture of the landform itself or of something that is related to the landform, such as a plant or animal that lives near or on it.

After each person has finished, display the pictures and information on a map of the world. Make a border around the map with the pictures and paragraphs and attach each one to its exact location with yarn and thumbtacks.

Crack, Crumble, and Carry

By conducting a variety of simple demonstrations, your group can discover more about how the forces of weathering, erosion, and deposition are constantly shaping the surface of the Earth. And afterward, they can take a hike to find examples of these processes at work in their community.

Before you begin, run off a copy of the demonstrations on page 38, cut them apart, and glue each one to an index card. Then briefly discuss the processes of weathering, erosion, and deposition using the information on pages 31-33.

After your discussion, divide the group into teams of four or five children and give each team one of the demonstration cards. Explain that each person on each team must conduct the demonstration on the card and record the results. Tell the kids that they should share materials.

Then explain that the members of each team should pool their information and put together a team presentation for the rest of the group. Tell the kids that each team's presentation should include the following:

1. An explanation of what they did, including a list of the materials they used, how they set up the demonstrations, what controls they used, and so on.
2. A discussion of the results of their demonstrations and what conclusions they drew from their results. They should also explain how their demonstration relates to weathering, erosion, or deposition.
3. An explanation of why some of the data that each person gathered differed (if it did), even though each person did the same demonstration.
4. A description of another way to demonstrate the same concept.

You should also mention that these are indoor demonstrations that simulate some of the processes of weathering, erosion, and deposition, and they are not exactly what happens outside. For example, explain that some of the materials used in the demonstrations, such as vinegar, lemon juice, and hydrogen peroxide, aren't the actual substances that would cause rocks to weather. But these chemicals act in a similar way to the ones that do shape the landscape.

Explain that each group can show the actual materials from the demonstration, conduct the demonstration in front of the group if it's a quick one, make charts or graphs to record their data, or use a flip chart to explain what happened. Also encourage each person in each team to take part in the team's presentation.

As the groups make their presentations, encourage the other children to ask questions or challenge the conclusions. Use the information under "What Should Have Happened" on page 39 to help with each discussion. Afterward, take the group on an erosion and weathering walk to see these processes in action.

Note: Some of these activities require more time than others and some require that the kids do part of the demonstration at home. So allow several days for all the demonstrations to be completed before having the teams share their results and conclusions. You can also cut down on the number of demonstrations or do them as class demonstrations to save on materials and time.

(continued next page)

Luise Woelflein

#1: Plaster and Ice

What You Need: plaster of Paris, water, a small balloon, two empty pint milk cartons (bottom halves only), a freezer

What To Do:
1. Fill the balloon with water until it is about the size of a Ping-Pong ball and tie a knot in the end.
2. Mix water with plaster of Paris until the mixture is as thick as yogurt. Pour half of the plaster in one milk carton and the other half in the other.
3. Push the balloon down into the plaster in one carton until it is about ¼ inch under the surface. Hold the balloon there until the plaster sets enough so that the balloon doesn't rise to the surface.
4. Let the plaster harden for about 1 hour.
5. Put both milk cartons in the freezer overnight.
6. Remove the containers the next day to see what happened.

What To Think About: What happened to the plaster that contained the balloon? What happened to the plaster that had no balloon? Why is there a difference? Which carton acted as the control? Why? How does this experiment show what happens when water seeps into a crack in a rock and freezes?

#2: A Sour Trick

What You Need: lemon juice, vinegar, medicine droppers, and two pieces each of limestone, calcite, chalk, and quartz

What To Do:
1. Put a few drops of lemon juice on four of the rock samples.
2. Put a few drops of vinegar on each of the four other rock samples. (Share the rock samples with all team members.)
3. Look and listen carefully each time you add vinegar or lemon juice.

What To Think About: What happens when you put lemon juice on each rock? What happens when you put vinegar on each rock? Did the lemon juice and vinegar act the same way on each rock? Why did some of the rocks react differently? What does this experiment have to do with weathering?

#3: Steel Wool and Water

What You Need: 3 shallow dishes, 3 pieces of steel wool, salt, water

What To Do:
1. Place each piece of steel wool in a shallow dish.
2. Pour equal amounts of water over 2 of the pieces of steel wool and leave the third piece dry.
3. Sprinkle one of these wet pieces with plenty of salt.
4. Observe and compare the 3 pieces every day for a week.

What To Think About: What happened to each piece of steel wool? Which piece changed the most? Why do you think the steel wool changed? Which piece of steel wool acted as the control? What does this experiment have to do with weathering?

#4: A Penny for Your Thoughts

What You Need: 4 new pennies, 4 shallow dishes, salt, vinegar, hydrogen peroxide, a hand lens, masking tape, a pen, a measuring spoon

What To Do:
1. Put each penny in a shallow dish, head-side up.
2. Cover 1 penny with 3 teaspoons of salt.
3. Cover another penny with 3 teaspoons of salt and 3 teaspoons of vinegar.
4. Cover the third penny with 3 teaspoons of salt, 3 teaspoons of vinegar, and 2 teaspoons of hydrogen peroxide.
5. Leave the fourth penny uncovered.
6. Label the dishes according to what you added to each penny.
7. Let the pennies stand for 2 or 3 days. Then clean them off and compare them, using a hand lens to get a close-up look.

What To Think About: How did the pennies in each dish change? Did some of the pennies change more than others? What do you think would happen if you left the pennies for another week? Which penny acted as the control? Why? Pennies are made of copper and zinc, which are two elements that are found in many kinds of rocks. Does this demonstration explain how these two elements weather? Why?

#5: Shake It Up

What You Need: 15 rough, jagged stones that are all about the same size, 3 containers with lids (such as coffee cans), 3 clear cups or jars, a pen, paper, masking tape

What To Do:
1. Separate the stones into 3 piles of 5 and put each pile on a sheet of paper.
2. Label each pile A, B, and C. Label each can and jar A, B, and C.
3. Fill CAN A halfway with water and put in the stones from PILE A. Do the same with CAN B and PILE B, and CAN C and PILE C. Let the stones stand in the water overnight.
4. The next day, hold CAN A in both hands and shake it hard about 100 times.
5. Remove the stones from CAN A and pour the water into JAR A. Observe the stones and the water.
6. Give CAN B about 1000 shakes. (You can rest between shakes.) Remove these stones and pour the water into JAR B. Observe the stones. Also observe the water in JAR B.
7. Do not shake CAN C. Remove the stones and pour the water into JAR C. Observe the stones and the water.
8. Compare the 3 piles of stones and the 3 jars of water.

What To Think About: How do the piles of stones differ? Can you explain why? Which pile acted as the control? Why? How do the jars of water differ? How does this show what happens to stones that are knocked about in a fast-moving river or stream?

#6: Ice on the Move

What You Need: sand, several flat pieces of shale or limestone, ice cubes, 2 paper towels, water, ice cube tray, a freezer

What To Do:
1. Mix several teaspoons of sand with water, and pour the mixture into ice cube trays and freeze.
2. Use a paper towel to pick up one of the sandy ice cubes.
3. Hold the ice tightly against a piece of shale or limestone and slowly push it across the rock several times.
4. Examine the surface of the rock.
5. Do the same thing with a regular ice cube on another piece of rock.

What To Think About: How do the rock surfaces compare? From what you know about glaciers, how does this experiment explain how glaciers help shape the land? Explain your answer.

#7: The Layered Jar

What You Need: large jar with a lid, water, pebbles or gravel, coarse sand, soil

What To Do:
1. Put a layer of pebbles, sand, and soil in the jar.
2. Fill the jar with water and cover it.
3. Shake the jar until everything in the water is jostled about.
4. Set the jar down and watch what happens, on and off, for about an hour. Then check it several hours later.

What To Think About: How did the water look after you shook the jar? Which material settled to the bottom first? Why? Which material settled last? Why? Based on this experiment, when a fast-flowing river carrying pebbles, sand, and soil begins to slow down, what will settle out first? What will be carried the farthest?

WHAT SHOULD HAVE HAPPENED

1. Plaster and Ice: The plaster containing the balloon should have cracked as the water in the balloon froze and expanded. Explain that when water seeps into cracks in rocks and freezes, it can eventually break rocks apart.

2. A Sour Trick: The lemon juice and vinegar both contain weak acids. The lemon juice contains citric acid and the vinegar contains acetic acid. These mild acids can dissolve rocks that contain calcium carbonate. The lemon juice and vinegar should have bubbled or fizzed on the limestone, calcite, and chalk, which all contain calcium carbonate. There should not have been a reaction on the quartz, which does not contain calcium carbonate. Explain that water often contains weak acids that dissolve rocks containing calcium carbonate and other minerals.

3. Steel Wool and Water: When iron gets wet, the water acts as an agent to speed up oxidation. (Oxidation occurs when oxygen combines with another substance.) In this case, oxygen in the water combined with the iron in the steel wool to form iron oxide, or rust. Rust is a weaker material than the original metal and erodes quickly. When salt is added to the water, it speeds up the oxidation of iron. So the steel wool in salt water will be the one that changes most.

4. A Penny for Your Thoughts: If the pennies are left long enough, the pennies with salt, salt and vinegar, and salt, vinegar, and hydrogen peroxide should all change. But the one with salt, vinegar, and hydrogen peroxide should change the most. Salt will react chemically with the copper to produce copper

chloride. Vinegar and salt will slowly dissolve the copper, forming green copper salts. And hydrogen peroxide will speed up the reaction, making the penny with vinegar, salt, and hydrogen peroxide corrode the fastest.

5. Shake It Up: The stones that were shaken up should have more rounded edges than the stones that weren't shaken. And the stones in CAN B should have rounder edges than the ones in CAN A. Both jars should have some sediment in the bottom, but JAR B should have more since more shakes would have broken off more bits of rock. The same thing happens to rocks that are carried along in rivers or are churned about by the surf.

6. Ice on the Move: The ice cube with sand acts like sandpaper, and should leave scratches on the rock surfaces. The control should not be scratched. When glaciers move across land, they pick up and move rock material. And some of this rock material can scratch and gouge rock surfaces.

7. The Layered Jar: When the jar is first shaken, the water appears cloudy. As the particles settle, the water becomes clearer. First the heaviest material—the pebbles or gravel—settles to the bottom. Then the sand settles out. And finally the lightest material—the clay and silt in the soil—settles on top. When a river slows down, the same thing happens, with the heavy boulders and rocks dropping out first and the fine silt and clay being dumped last. This is why a fertile delta often forms at the mouth of a river.

PART 2: A WEAR-IT-AWAY WALK

After the children have a better understanding of how the Earth's wearing-down and building-up forces work, take them on a hike to look for signs of weathering, erosion, and deposition in the neighborhood. Here are some suggestions:

- Look for signs of erosion caused by water on bare hillsides and slopes. Also look on the banks of rivers or streams and near construction sites where trees and grass have been removed. (Plants help slow down erosion.)
- On a rainy day, check for soil washing away under storm drains.
- Look for places where trees and other plants are growing out of rocks, such as plants growing through a

crack in a sidewalk. Look for bits of soil in the cracks.

- Look for lichens on rocks. Explain that lichens can start to grow in rock crevices, and as they grow they produce a mild acid which can help break rocks down.
- Look at the tombstones in a graveyard for signs of weathering. Have parts of the rocks changed colors (sometimes indicating a chemical reaction), cracked, or broken apart? Do older tombstones show more evidence of weathering?
- Look for smooth rocks in stream beds and on beaches.
- Look for loose rock and soil at the bases of slopes.

People

Plants

cut

cut

Snow and Ice

Animals

Undersea Mountains

Volcanoes

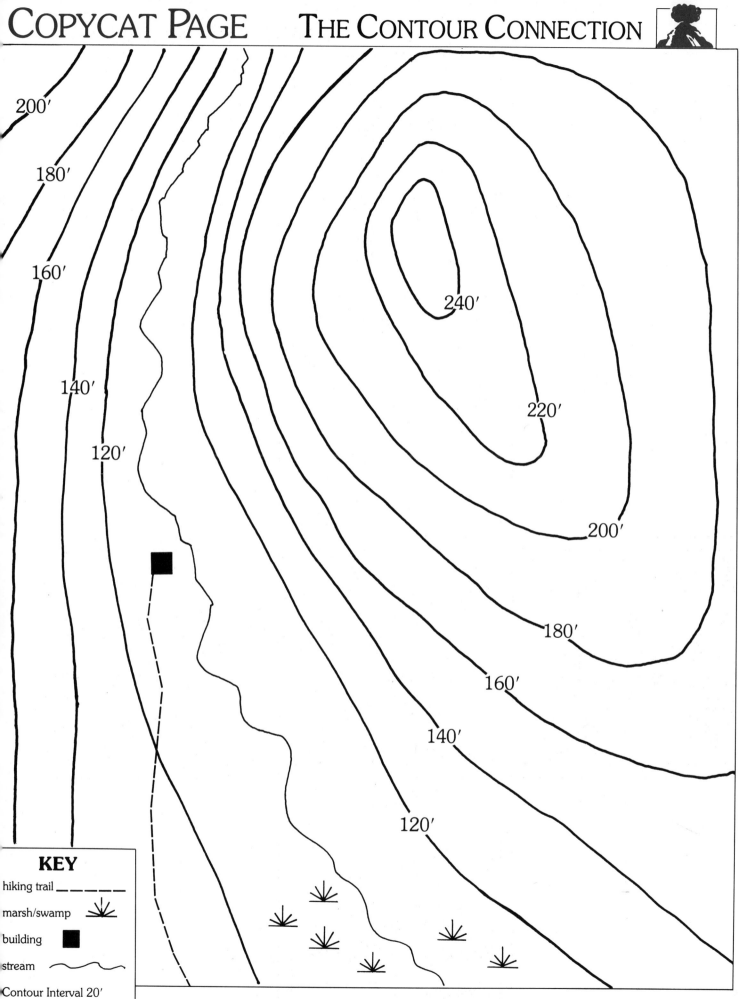

200'
180'
160'
140'
120'

240'
220'
200'
180'
160'
140'
120'

KEY

hiking trail   — — — —

marsh/swamp   ☀

building   ■

stream   ∿

Contour Interval 20'

RANGER RICK'S NATURESCOPE: GEOLOGY—THE ACTIVE EARTH

SECRETS OF THE PAST

T remendous numbers of organisms have lived and died on our planet since life first evolved several billion years ago. Of these, only a small percentage have survived the ages as fossils. Fossils are any remains of ancient life, from huge dinosaur skeletons, to microscopic grains of pollen, to animal tracks and trails.

These ancient bits and pieces, along with the rocks many of them are embedded in, have revealed a lot about the history of life on Earth. And they've been invaluable in telling us what our planet has been like through the ages: sometimes warm and lush, sometimes cold and harsh—but always changing.

A FIRST LOOK AT FOSSILS

Set in Stone: Most of the remains and traces of organisms that eventually became fossilized didn't survive the ages in their original form. One reason for this is that the soft parts of a "potential fossil" (organs and so on) usually decay or get eaten by scavengers soon after the organism dies. So in general only an organism's hard parts—woody tissue, teeth, and bones, for example—become preserved. (There are a few examples of fossil algae and other "softies," but these formed under very special circumstances that don't often occur during fossilization.)

The parts of organisms that don't decay often change to stone over time. Generally this happens as chemical-laden water partially or completely dissolves away and replaces the bone, wood, or other original material of a fossil-in-the-making. (For more about the different types of fossils and how they form, see pages 34-35 of *NatureScope—Digging Into Dinosaurs* [Vol. 1, No. 2].)

Sunken in Sediment: Most fossils are embedded in rock, and the rock they're embedded in is almost always sedimentary. The reason for this has a lot to do with the way sedimentary rock forms: If, when an organism dies, it's quickly covered by a layer of sand, silt, or other fine sediment, it will be much more protected from scavengers and decomposers than if it were left exposed. So fast burial by sediment sets the stage for fossilization. As time passes, more and more layers may cover the organism—and eventually the layers may harden into sedimentary rock.

Unlike sedimentary rock, igneous and metamorphic rock aren't good sources of fossils. In the case of igneous rock, would-be fossils are often burned up when they're covered by lava. And the changes rocks go through during metamorphism usually destroy any fossils that may originally have been contained in them. (For more about the three basic types of rock and how they form, see "One of the Family" on page 19.)

Where Fossils Form: If, many millions of years from now, scientists were to study the geology of the Rocky Mountains, they might not discover that mountain goats, pikas, and other animals were once common Rocky Mountain residents. That's because animals don't stand much of a chance of becoming fossilized in mountainous areas. The steep mountain landscape doesn't allow much sediment to build up—so mountain organisms usually aren't buried in layers of mud, sand, silt, or other sediment when they die. In places such as deltas and the bottoms of lakes and slow-moving rivers, on the other hand, sediment builds up readily. That's one reason that fossils of aquatic organisms are so much more abundant than those of land organisms.

Moving Up in the World: Despite the fact that mountains aren't good

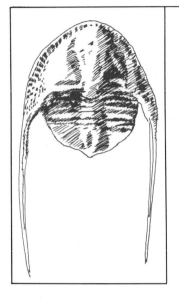

Forever Amber: Although scenarios such as that portrayed in the movie "Jurassic Park" are unlikely, scientists have discovered that fossils trapped in amber may be a promising source of DNA of organisms that are now extinct. Amber is the fossilized resin of trees. Insects and small organisms were occasionally trapped in the resin as it seeped out of trees. Some amber fossils date back 310 million years, to Carboniferous times. The soft tissues (organs and so on) of fossils in amber are often intact, providing DNA information. Fossils in amber may also help scientists fill in the gaps in the fossil record. Although amber is found throughout most of the Earth, the greatest deposits are in the area of the Baltic Sea and the Dominican Republic.

"nurseries" for fossils, the rocks found in mountains are often loaded with the remains of ancient life. But these fossils formed when the landscape was much different from what it is today. Before the Appalachian Mountains were uplifted, for example, a shallow sea stretched hundreds of miles inland over what is now eastern and midwestern North America. Some of the fossils formed in the sediment of this shallow sea and are now exposed in certain rock layers of the Appalachians.

PUTTING THE PIECES TOGETHER

Before the mid-1800s, one popular explanation for "phenomena" such as fossils of marine organisms on mountaintops was that the organisms had been deposited there during the Great Flood of Noah's time. People assumed that oceans, mountains, and other features of the Earth's surface had always existed in the same place, and evidence to the contrary wasn't yet recognized. But as the science of geology got underway, and paleontologists began to understand fossil "clues," new ideas about the Earth and how it works slowly began to fall into place.

Ages of the Ancient: In the early 1900s an important technique was developed that revolutionized paleontology and geology as a whole. This technique, called *radiometric dating,* is based on the observation that radioactive elements called *radioisotopes* break down into other elements at a fixed rate. By measuring the amounts of different elements in a given rock, figuring out what proportion of the radioisotopes have broken down into other elements, and determining how long it would have taken this breakdown to occur, geologists can calculate the age of the rock with a high degree of accuracy.

Rock Sandwiches: Scientists often use radiometric dating to figure out the ages of fossils too—but usually only in an indirect way. Radiometric dating is most effective with igneous rocks, and as we pointed out earlier, igneous rocks aren't good sources of fossils. Sedimentary rocks, on the other hand, often contain fossils, but radiometric dating isn't very useful with these rocks. That's because much of the radioactive material sedimentary rocks contain ultimately came from igneous rocks. And there's no way to determine when these radioactive fragments eroded from their igneous "parents" and finally became deposited in sediment.

So to find the ages of fossils—i.e., to figure out when organisms were trapped in the sediment they'd eventually become preserved in—scientists often look to see if the fossil-laden rock is sandwiched between layers of igneous rock. By using radiometric dating to figure out the ages of the igneous layers both above and below the fossil layer, scientists can reach a good age estimate of both the sedimentary layer and the fossils it contains.

Back to the Beginning: How far back into the history of life on Earth have dating techniques taken us? Probably pretty close to life's beginnings. The oldest fossils discovered so far are bacteria that, according to dating techniques, were probably alive about three and a half billion years ago. Scientists think that bacteria such as these were among the first organisms to evolve on the Earth. (Most scientists think that the Earth formed about 4.6 billion years ago, which means that it was probably a little more than a billion years old by the time life got started. For information about how scientists have categorized the history of life on Earth, see "Rock Detectives" on page 50. Also see pages 24-25 of *NatureScope—Digging Into Dinosaurs* [Vol. 1, No. 2].)

(continued next page)

Evolutionary Evidence: If it weren't for fossils, we might never have realized that life on Earth has gradually been changing, or *evolving*, since those first tiny bacteria took their stand so long ago. For a few species, such as the horse, an extensive evolutionary record has been preserved in the rocks. Scientists have found fossils of many stages in the horse's development—all the way back to a slender, four-toed beast no bigger than a greyhound. The fossil record isn't as complete for most organisms, but the principle of gradual change through time does show up for many of them.

When a species suddenly drops out of the fossil record altogether (i.e., when its fossils can't be found in the layers after a certain point), scientists can be reasonably sure that the species became extinct. For some reason, these species weren't able to meet the demands and stresses of a changing environment. The extinctions of the dinosaurs—and of many other organisms—have been recorded in this way.

Past Climates Revealed: The story fossils tell reaches way beyond a chronology of who lived when and how organisms changed through time. We've already talked about fossils as indicators of changes in the landscape, for example. (See "Moving Up in the World" on pages 42-43.) Another "variable" that fossils can reveal is climate. Just as now, each animal and plant of the past was adapted to living within a certain range of climatic conditions—dry, wet, hot, cold, or whatever. So by studying the kinds of fossils that characterize a certain area, paleontologists can get a handle on the climatic changes that have taken place. Over the years, some dramatic shifts have occurred. For example, fossils of tropical plants have been found in the rocks of Antarctica. And caribou and other cold-loving animals once lived on tundra that existed as far south as what is now Tennessee.

Born in the U.S.A.?: It's interesting to think about plants and animals once populating areas that aren't anywhere near the organisms' present ranges. Take camels, for example. Today they're desert animals of Africa and Asia. But a couple of million years ago their ancestors were roaming the grasslands of what is now the American West. You could say, then, that camels are bona fide Native Americans, right up there with the American bison. And it would be hard to get much more American than that.

Or would it? Actually, bison didn't originate in the land they've come to symbolize. Their ancestors arose in Asia, and they migrated to North America when landmasses were connected in places that are now flooded by oceans. Camels, on the other hand, eventually disappeared from North America completely. (Some camel relatives did stay in the New World, though. That's why there are alpacas, llamas, guanacos, and vicuñas in South America today.)

The fact that animals have moved around so much through the ages indicates that the Earth's landmasses haven't stood still. Plate tectonics has created and destroyed avenues to new areas, dictating where animals and plants can live. And sea level changes have created and destroyed bridges between landmasses. (See pages 4-5 for information on plate tectonics.) But how do scientists know, for example, where camels and bison originated and where they ended up?

Links with the Past: Fossils and the rocks they're buried in reveal secrets such as these—just as they have revealed secrets about past climates, landscapes, evolution, geography, and so on. By correctly interpreting these fossil clues and using radiometric dating and other techniques to help them reach conclusions, paleontologists can track the development and movements of organisms through the eons.

Of course, unless we can someday travel back in time, we'll never know all there is to know about the Earth's distant past and the animals and plants that have populated the planet. But each new find adds a little more "color" to the picture. And there will always be "new" fossils, just waiting to be discovered.

Changing Times

orth America hasn't always looked as it does today. In the past 600 million years parts of it have been submerged under shallow seas, covered by tropical forests, and buried under thick sheets of ice. This activity will focus on some of the ways one state—Wyoming—has changed since prehistoric times.

Begin by pointing out Wyoming on a map of the United States. (Even if you live in Wyoming, locating the state will give your group a better idea of where it is located in relation to the rest of the country.) Ask the kids to tell you what they know about the wildlife, landscape, climate, and plant life of Wyoming. Then fill in the gaps, showing pictures of Wyoming and using the following information about the state:

- is mostly flat and covered by grasses and scattered trees
- gets very little rainfall
- is bordered by rugged mountains
- has warm summers and cold winters
- has bighorn sheep, moose, mule deer, elk, pronghorn antelope, prairie dogs, bison, bald eagles, golden eagles, thrushes, trout, and many other wild animals

mammoth

Next tell the kids that Wyoming, along with the rest of North America, has not always looked the way it does today, and that many different kinds of animals once lived there. Pass out a copy of page 53 to each person and tell the kids that the pictures on the left-hand side of the page show how Wyoming might have looked at different times long, long ago. Have the kids look at the pictures as you use the information below to describe what the climate and land were like in each time period.

Picture 1: About 550 million years ago, a warm, shallow sea stretched across much of North America, including Wyoming. Jellyfish, sea worms, and many other sea creatures were common. But fish, turtles, and many other animals that live in the seas today had not yet appeared.

Picture 2: Millions of years later, the seas had dried up and tropical forests covered much of the land. The temperatures were warm throughout the year. And many new forms of life had appeared, including fish, birds, reptiles, mammals, and flowering plants.

Picture 3: About 100,000 years ago, the temperatures in North America were much colder. Most of the tropical forests had died out and had been replaced by plants that could live in cold temperatures. In the coldest areas of the north, snow began to pile up on the ground, forming thick layers. Over time this snow turned into huge sheets of ice that covered much of North America. Some animals died out during these frigid times. But others adapted to the colder climate.

Now tell the kids that each of the animals on the right-hand side of the page lived in one of these time periods. None of them is alive today, but scientists have figured out what the animals looked like from studying the *fossils* they left behind. Using the background information on pages 42-44, briefly explain what fossils are and how they form.

Point out to the kids that the animals that lived in each time period were specially suited to the climate and landforms of that time. Ask the kids to decide which time period each animal lived in and to draw a line to match each animal with that period. (You can also do this as a group discussion.) Then use the information below to go over the kids' answers and explain how each animal was suited to where it lived.

Mammoth (A) belongs in Picture 3. This animal had thick underfur and long outer hairs that kept it warm. It was as big as an elephant. It used its long tusks to dig grass and other plant foods from beneath the snow.

Trilobites (B) belong in Picture 1. Most of these animals were smaller than your hand and lived in the ancient oceans. They had a hard outer covering (called an exoskeleton) just as crabs, insects, and many other animals have today. They had many legs, which they used like paddles to move through the water and to crawl along the seafloor. Most of them ate bits of dead plant and animal material.

Triceratops (C) belongs in Picture 2. This dinosaur was well protected from enemies. Its body was covered with tough, thick skin and it had three sharp horns on its head to help defend itself. This animal was a plant eater and often traveled in herds like many other plant-eating dinosaurs.

Next pass out markers and crayons, construction paper, scissors, and glue. Have the kids color the pictures, then cut out the time-period and animal pictures along the solid lines. Have them glue the time-period pictures onto a piece of construction paper and then glue each animal in the correct time period. You can also have the kids draw pictures of a few of the plants and animals that live in Wyoming today.

Official State Fossils

Learn about your state's official fossil, or elect your own state fossil.

Objective:
Name your state fossil (or another fossil found in your state) and talk about what makes the fossil special.

Ages:
Primary, Intermediate, and Advanced

Materials:
- *reference books*
- *poster paper, markers, crayons, paints, and other art supplies (optional)*

Subjects:
Science and Art

ossils deserve a lot of credit. After all, if it weren't for fossils, we'd never know that dinosaurs weighing five times as much as an African elephant once browsed their way across the landscape. And the word *evolution* might never have become part of our vocabulary.

Here's a way for your group to give fossils some special recognition. Start by asking if anyone knows what your state bird, tree, or flower is. Explain that many states have other mascots too, such as a state insect or a state mammal. And some states even have state fossils! (To find out if your state has an official fossil, check your local library for a listing of state symbols.) If your state has a fossil, have the kids research it to find out all they can about it. You could also have them make models and posters or write poems and songs about the fossil. (See "Does Your State Have a Fossil?" *Ranger Rick*, November 1986, pp 11-13, for more about the state fossils of California, Colorado, Montana, Nebraska, and Nevada.)

If your state doesn't have an official fossil, you might want to have your group organize a campaign to designate one. Tell the kids that a sixth-grade class in Livingston, Montana, did just that by writing letters to state legislators and collecting nearly 9000 signatures on a petition. The letters and petition supported making *Maiasaura* (MY-ah-SAWR-ah), a duck-billed dinosaur, the official state fossil. The class got to see their state's government in action when they attended a hearing on the matter, and all of their involvement eventually paid off: In 1985 the Montana government designated *Maiasaura* as the official state fossil.

The kids in your group don't have to go all the way to the state government, though. Instead, you can simply have them vote on the fossil they think would be best for the state. (How about having them make "campaign buttons" and hold a school-wide election?) The kids can use any criteria they want in electing a state fossil, but here are some things they might want to keep in mind:
- the fossil's abundance in the state

- whether the fossil is unique to the state
- whether the fossil has any unusual features
- whether the fossil indicates some kind of change in the state through time (a shift in climate or change in landscape, for example)

You could also hold a special fossil day. For an activity the kids can do on that day, see "Rock Detectives" on page 50. And for an outdoor fossil activity, try "The Tooth, Claw, and Bone Mystery Hunt" on page 40 of *NatureScope—Digging Into Dinosaurs* (Vol. 1, No. 2).

A Far-Out Filmstrip

Make a pull-through filmstrip that shows how some animals have changed through time.

Objectives:
Name two animals that once lived in prehistoric North America. Describe two ways that land bridges affected the evolution of animal life.

Ages:
Intermediate and Advanced

Materials:
- ***copies of pages 54 and 55***
- ***copies of the captions on page 50***
- ***construction paper***
- ***rulers***
- ***glue***
- ***scissors***
- ***tape***
- ***stapler***
- ***crayons or markers***
- ***bell (optional)***

Subject:
Science

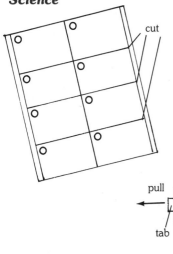

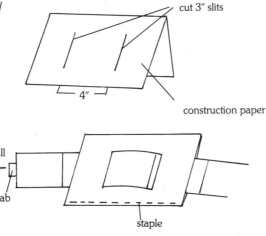

hich of these animals are native to North America—rhinoceroses or camels? If you answered *both,* you're right! In this activity your kids will learn more about these and other animals that once lived in North America by listening to the narration of an "alien filmstrip."

Begin by passing out a copy of page 55 to everyone. Then use the background information on page 50 of "Rock Detectives" to discuss how the history of the Earth is divided into major time divisions called *eras.* Have the kids look at the events on the Copycat Page to see how life on Earth has changed during each era.

Next tell the kids that they'll be focusing on the changes that occurred in North America during the Cenozoic Era. But they'll be looking at this era from an unusual viewpoint—that of an alien from another planet.

Tell the kids to imagine that scientists on Earth have just intercepted a broadcast from a meeting of top biologists on Hrundria (Ha-RUN-dree-a), a planet in a distant galaxy. Explain that they'll be seeing and hearing a translation of a presentation given by one of the Hrundrian biologists who have been studying the Earth for millions of years.

To get ready for the show, pass out copies of page 54, two 8½ × 11-inch (20 × 28-cm) pieces of construction paper, rulers, crayons or markers, glue, tape, and scissors, and have the kids follow these directions:

1. Color the pictures on the Copycat Page.
2. Cover the back of the Copycat Page with a *thin* layer of glue. Glue the page in the center of one of the pieces of construction paper.
3. Cut along the solid horizontal lines only.
4. Tape the four strips together by matching up the letters on the tabs at the ends of each strip. (Tape the front and back of each strip so the pictures will slide easily through the viewers.)
5. Cut out a 2½-inch (6.3-cm) long and 1½-inch (3.8-cm) wide construction paper tab and tape it to the left-hand end of the strip (on frame 1).
6. Fold the construction paper in half and make two vertical 3-inch (7.5-cm) slits 4 inches (10 cm) apart (see diagram).
7. Starting with frame 1, insert the left-hand end of the strip into the viewer (see diagram).
8. Staple the bottom edge of the viewer.

Then pass out a copy of the captions on page 50 to each person and give the kids time to read them. Explain that you will be reading the alien biologist's presentation (on the next page). And as you read, they will be pulling their strips through the viewers and following along. As they listen to the narration for each frame they should choose the caption that best fits the frame and write that frame number next to the caption. Each time you reach a new frame in the narration, you can ring a bell or make some other noise to signal that it's time to move to the next frame.

Frame 1: Here, fellow Hrundrians, is a picture of the Earth as it looked 54 million years ago. As you can see, there were several landmasses surrounded by salty oceans. The temperature was warm almost everywhere on the planet.

The star marks the site of my base on one of the northern landmasses. I returned several times during my 54-million-year study. In my study, I focused on some of the animals that lived on this landmass and how they changed over time.

At this time, the two northern landmasses were connected to each other by land bridges. These bridges are shaded on the map. Later I'll talk more about the importance of land bridges and how they changed during my study.

Frame 2: Here's a close-up of two different kinds of animals I saw on my first trip to Earth. They lived among the low bushes of the tropical forests that covered the landmass. Both had four toes on each foot that spread apart and helped them walk on the soft forest floor. They ate twigs and leaves. And neither of them was bigger than a quagendrat. (*Note: A quagendrat is a Hrundrian animal about the size of an Irish setter.*) I called the one in the foreground an esroh. But many millions of years later, I learned that humans called them the ancestors of their "horses." I named the one in the background a blatot, but humans would call it the forerunner of "rhinoceroses."

Frame 3: Several million years later, I returned to the same area. The climate was still warm and thick forests still covered the landscape.

These two animals were common. After several years of study, I decided that the animal in the foreground had evolved from the esroh, or horse ancestor, I showed earlier. I observed that it was larger than the esroh in frame 2 and had only three toes on each front foot.

I named the other animal in this picture a lemac and noticed that it also browsed on plants. It was about the size of the animal humans now call a "sheep."

Frame 4: I saw these two animals on the same trip. I believe they were distant relatives of the modern-day rhinoceroses. They lived mostly in swampy wooded areas and near streams. One was large and very heavy, and the other was slender and could run very fast.

Frame 5: After fifteen million years back home on Hrundria, I returned to my base camp on Earth. The climate was cooler and drier—especially in the north. There were many open, grassy areas, and the forests were not as thick as they had been.

The horses I saw, like the one in the picture, now had one large toe with two small toes instead of three small ones on each foot. They placed most of their weight on the large toe. This "new" foot design seemed more suited for walking and running on the harder ground.

The lemac on the left had two toes on each foot, as the earlier lemacs did. It could run fast on its long, slender legs. I decided lemacs were the ancestors of what humans now call "camels."

Frame 6: About 12 million years later, when I returned to Earth, grasslands covered the northern landmass. The camels and horses I saw were well adapted to the open, grassy areas. The camel in the foreground was very tall—tall enough to look into the second-floor window of a modern Earth building. The horse had one toe per foot, and could run faster than the earlier horses.

During this trip I noticed that a land bridge had formed between the northern and southern landmasses. Many different kinds of animals moved between the two landmasses on this land bridge. I observed some early camels and horses traveling from the northern landmass to the southern landmass across this bridge.

I didn't see any rhinos on the northern landmass, or any crossing the land bridge into the southern landmass. I believe that they couldn't survive on a diet of "new," tough grasses that grew in the cooler northern climate. They must have died out (at least on this northern landmass) before the land bridge had formed.

Frame 7: I returned for one of my last visits one and a half million years ago—and was I glad that I'd brought my ungilick furs! This map shows the boundaries of the great ice sheets that covered the northern regions of the landmasses. During this time, the ocean levels were lowered and wide land bridges—wider than before—reached between some of the landmasses.

Frame 8: These are pictures of some of the animals I saw on this cold trip. I guessed that their ancestors had crossed onto the landmass where I was based from

the other northern landmass. These animals were well adapted to the cold temperatures and grazed on the open areas south of the ice sheets.

This is the final entry in my report. Ten thousand years ago, I gathered additional data with my long-range scanning sensor. (I wish that thing had been invented earlier—it would have saved me a lot of trips to Earth!) I found that at this time, horses no longer lived on the landmass where I set up base (now known as North America). But I did see them on some of the other landmasses. I detected rhinos only on the landmasses humans now call Asia and Africa. And there were no members of the camel family living on North America where camels first orig-

inated. Instead, my sensor indicated that members of the camel family were living in Asia and Africa, and on the landmass known as South America.

After careful analysis of my data, I can now explain the disappearance of camels and horses about 10,000 years ago from North America. The extinction of camels and horses was due to . . .

Unfortunately, the alien biologist's report was cut off by cosmic static—just before he explained a mystery that has puzzled scientists on Earth for many years.

In your follow-up discussion, you can talk about this "mystery" along with the following questions about the filmstrip. (Also go over the captions and the pictures each one goes with.)

- How did horses change over time? (They became larger, ate different types of plants, and changed from having several toes to having only one large toe per foot.) How do you think Earth scientists learned about these changes? (Scientists learned about the evolution of the horse by studying fossils.)
- Explain the importance of land bridges in relation to the evolution of animals. (Land bridges allowed animals to expand into new habitats as their populations grew. Some kinds of animals became extinct when they were forced to compete with other animals.)
- Name some of the things that influenced which animals survived. (climate and resulting changes in vegetation)
- Do you know the names of one or more members of the camel family that now live in South America? (llamas, alpacas, guanacos, and vicuñas)
- Can you give a reason why the mammals of Australia are so different from ones in other parts of the world? (Australia was separated from the other landmasses early in the development of mammals. Many unique mammals evolved in this isolated habitat.)

Finally, explain that scientists still aren't sure why camels, horses, and rhinos became extinct in North America. They think camels and horses could have died out due to a change in vegetation, competition from other grazers (deer and bison that migrated from Asia), or over-hunting by early people who appeared in North America about 12,000 years ago. (Horses didn't reappear in North America until Spanish explorers reintroduced them.) And rhinos could have become extinct because of a change in climate and/or vegetation.

CAPTIONS

A. Two different species of rhino-relatives lived in swampy areas.
B. Horses now ate grasses instead of twigs and leaves, and camels had longer legs.
C. During the ice ages, wide land bridges formed when sea levels dropped.
D. The first horses and rhinoceroses were adapted to living in tropical forests.

E. Some animals had thick hair that helped them survive in cold climates.
F. More than 50 million years ago, the two northern landmasses were connected by land bridges.
G. Early horses and "lemacs" lived in forests and browsed on twigs and leaves.
H. Camels and horses traveled across land bridges to other landmasses.

Answers: frame 1—F; frame 2—D; frame 3—G; frame 4—A; frame 5—B; frame 6—H; frame 7—C; frame 8—E.

Rock Detectives

Use clues to solve some fossil brain teasers.

Objectives:
Describe how fossils can reveal information about the past. Talk about some of the techniques paleontologists use to answer questions about the history of life on Earth.

Ages:
Advanced

Materials:
- ***copies of pages 55, 56, and 57***
- ***list of questions provided in the activity***
- ***chalkboard or easel paper***
- ***paper***
- ***pencils***

Subjects:
Science and Math

aleontologists are a lot like detectives: They try to solve mysteries by discovering clues and interpreting them in the right way. Unlike most detectives, though, paleontologists deal with mysteries of the past—some of which are millions of years old!

Your kids can do a little of their own paleontological detective work by using clues to answer questions about hypothetical layers of rock. But before they begin "investigating," copy the questions on page 52 (but not the answers) onto a sheet of paper. (Keep in mind that this activity will work best if your group already has a good geology background.) Run off enough copies of this sheet for everyone, then put them aside. Next use the background information on pages 42-44 and 17-19 to talk about fossils, the Earth's past, and the different kinds of rocks and how they form. Also go over the information in "The Lowdown on Radioactive Breakdown" (on the next page) to help the kids understand radiometric dating.

Now pass out copies of page 55 and have the kids follow along as you discuss geologic time. Explain that scientists have divided the history of life on Earth into *eras*. Each era is based on the type of life that was abundant at that time. For example, the Mesozoic Era (also called The Age of Dinosaurs) is characterized by the giant reptiles that "ruled" the planet for about 160 million years. You might want to point out that, so far, people have been around for only a short time: less than five million years!

Now copy the diagram in the margin onto a chalkboard or piece of easel paper and explain that scientists have calculated the Earth's age to be about 4.6 billion years. Point out that the Precambrian Era lasted for the first four billion years of the Earth's history. Although scientists don't know much about it, they do know that the first simple lifeforms developed during this time. Also compare the lengths of the Paleozoic, Mesozoic, and Cenozoic Eras on the diagram and point out that the eras on the Copycat Page are not drawn to scale. If they were, the Cenozoic Era would not have enough room for pictures. (For more about geologic time and the Paleozoic, Mesozoic, and Cenozoic Eras, see pages 24-33 of *Nature-Scope—Digging Into Dinosaurs* [Vol. 1, No. 2].)

Cenozoic Era
Mesozoic Era
Paleozoic Era
Precambrian Era

After your discussion, pass out a copy of page 57 to each person. Give the kids a few minutes to read through the clues. Explain that the plant and animal fossils pictured are all fictitious. So are the gamlonia tree mentioned in the first clue and the fakium and hokium mentioned in the fourth clue. But all of the scientific concepts, such as adaptation, extinction, and radioactive breakdown, are real.

Next pass out copies of page 56. Tell the kids that the layers on the page represent a cross-section of rock strata with fossils in them. Explain that the pictures aren't drawn to scale—for example, the dinosaur footprints would be much larger than we've pictured them. Also, fossils in real rock usually wouldn't be positioned as they are in the picture. (Instead, most would be lying flat—parallel to the surface of the ground.) And whole animal and plant fossils aren't commonly found. But we've pictured the strata and fossils this way so we could fit in a lot of information.

Now pass out the question sheets you ran off earlier. Tell the kids that all of the questions refer to page 56, and that they should use the list of clues and the time line (pages 57 and 55) to answer them. Have them answer the questions on a separate sheet of paper. They should include in their answers the numbers of the clues that support the answers and/or an explanation of any supportive information that they gleaned from the time line.

THE LOWDOWN ON RADIOACTIVE BREAKDOWN

As we pointed out in "Ages of the Ancient" on page 43, scientists can date layers of igneous rock by using radiometric dating techniques. The rate at which a radioisotope breaks down into other elements is measured in terms of its *half life*—i.e., the amount of time it takes for half of the radioisotope in a rock to break down. For example, uranium 235, a radioisotope of the element uranium, has a half life of about 700 million years. That means that it takes 700 million years for half of the original uranium 235 in a given sample of rock to break down. (Uranium 235 eventually breaks down into lead.)

After another 700 million years, half of the remaining uranium 235 will have gradually broken down into lead. In other words, after 1400 million years, only 25 percent of the original uranium 235 will remain in a given rock sample. This breakdown of uranium 235 (or any other radioisotope, for that matter) continues indefinitely—and eventually the amounts of radioisotopes can no longer be accurately measured.

(continued next page)

STRAIN YOUR BRAIN!

1. **Which of the following habitats was layer 1 a part of when it was laid down?**
   a. forest
   b. freshwater marsh
   c. desert
   d. seashore
   e. saltwater pond
   (d. Clue 12 lists two adaptations that an animal living along the shoreline of an ocean might have.)

2. **The scallop-like fossil in layers 2-5 is found in sediment all over the world. It's abundant everywhere it's found, but it always suddenly "drops out of the picture" after a certain point. What might have happened to the animal this fossil represents?** (The animal probably became extinct. Clue 16 points out that the animal is never found in sediment less than 450 million years old.)

3. **True or false: The rock in layers 6, 8, and 10 formed when sediment that had settled in the mouth of a river (or some other body of water) gradually was buried, pressed together, and cemented into rock.** (False. Clue 5 states that layers 6, 8, and 10 are made up of igneous rock. Igneous rock forms when magma cools and hardens.)

4. **In which layer would you expect to find the most coal? Explain your answer.** (Layer 7 would probably have the most coal since it contains the most fossils of the plant that, according to clue 10, grew in swamps that existed at the end of the Paleozoic Era. As page 55 portrays, this was when much of the Earth's coal formed.)

5. **The igneous rock that makes up layer 8 contains the radioisotope called "fakium." If 50 percent of the fakium in the layer has changed to "hokium," how old is the layer?** (300 million years old. Clue 4 says that the half life of fakium is 300 million years.)

6. **What might be one reason that the sea plant in layers 2-5 gradually evolved spines?** (Clue 19 pictures a fish that was abundant in shallow seas. The fish, a grazer, might have fed on the plants, and over time the plants might have evolved the spines as a defense against being eaten.

Point out to the kids that evolution isn't a conscious effort [i.e., the fish didn't consciously "put pressure on" the plant by eating it, and the plant didn't consciously develop spines to protect itself]. But over time, those plants that happened to have protective spines survived to reproduce, and those that didn't died out.)

7. **Look at layer 4 and compare the number of clockwise fossil snail shells to the number of counter-clockwise fossil shells. Based on your observations, what can you say about the climate of the area when layer 4 was laid down?** (Clue 14 states that the direction of the shell's spiral correlates with climate. Since there are more clockwise snails in layer 4, the climate was probably tropical in the area where the layers were being laid down.)

8. **True or false: Layers 6, 8, and 10 probably were located near a volcano or some other area where magma was rising.** (True. Clue 5 says that layers 6, 8, and 10 are made up of igneous rock, and igneous rock is formed when magma cools and hardens.)

9. **Look at the tracks in layer 9. If you were told that the tracks showed that the larger animal captured and ate the smaller one, would you believe it? Why or why not?** (Clue 2 says that the largest dinosaurs were vegetarians, clue 18 depicts the footprint of an 80-ton [72-t] dinosaur, and clue 11 depicts the footprint of a small, carnivorous dinosaur. The bigger dinosaur was a vegetarian, and so would not have captured and eaten the smaller one.)

10. **Based on the fact that the bone in layer 11 belonged to a dinosaur and that gamlonia trees were present at this time, which of the following statements is most accurate?**
    a. Layer 11 was laid down just as dinosaurs were getting started.
    b. Layer 11 was laid down about the time dinosaurs were starting to die out.
    c. Layer 11 was laid down during the middle of the dinosaurs' reign as the most dominant animals on Earth.

(b. Clue 1 says that gamlonia trees developed near the end of the Mesozoic. According to page 55, the Mesozoic Era ended about 65 million years ago. And clue 9 says that dinosaurs died out about 65 million years ago.)

11. **The fossil jawbone in layer 12 represents an animal whose remains are known from only one other location. This other location is thousands of miles away, on another continent. How would you explain how the fossils came to be located so far from each other? (Hint: Keep in mind that the world hasn't always looked as it does today!)** (Clue 8 says that many of the world's landmasses were once joined, but have since drifted apart as crustal plates have shifted. The animals represented by the jawbone could have been on the same landmass at one time, and then become separated when two plates split apart. The appearance and then disappearance of land bridges could also account for this. [For more about land bridges, see pages 47-49.])

12. **Do you think the animal whose fossil jaw is in layer 12 was a plant eater or a meat eater?** (The jaw is that of a plant eater. The kids can contrast this jaw to that shown in clue 13, which is the jaw of a carnivorous animal [a meat eater]).

13. **When layer 7 was forming, was the area a desert, ocean, swamp, tundra, or prairie? Explain your answer.** (Swamp. Clue 10 pictures a swamp plant, and there are plenty of these fossils in layer 7.)

14. **If the area in which all of the layers occur is now mountainous, would you say that the fossils in layer 12 probably formed before or after the mountains pushed up? Explain your answer.** (Before. Clue 3 discusses the fact that fossils form best in areas of high sedimentation, such as in shallow ocean areas and near the mouths of rivers. And clue 7 points out that, because there is so much erosion in mountains, not much sediment builds up in them.)

Picture 1

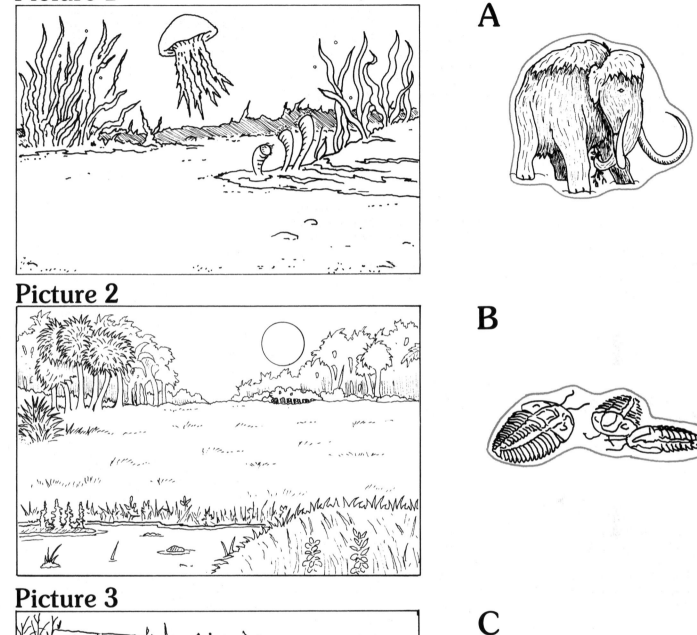

A

Picture 2

B

Picture 3

C

COPYCAT PAGE

A FAR-OUT FILMSTRIP

① land bridges

54 million years ago

② 54 million years ago

③ 30 million years ago

④ 30 million years ago

⑤ 15 million years ago

⑥ 3 million years ago

⑦ ice sheets

165,000 years ago

⑧ 165,000 years ago

A

B

C

COPYCAT PAGE ROCK DETECTIVES—SHEET 1

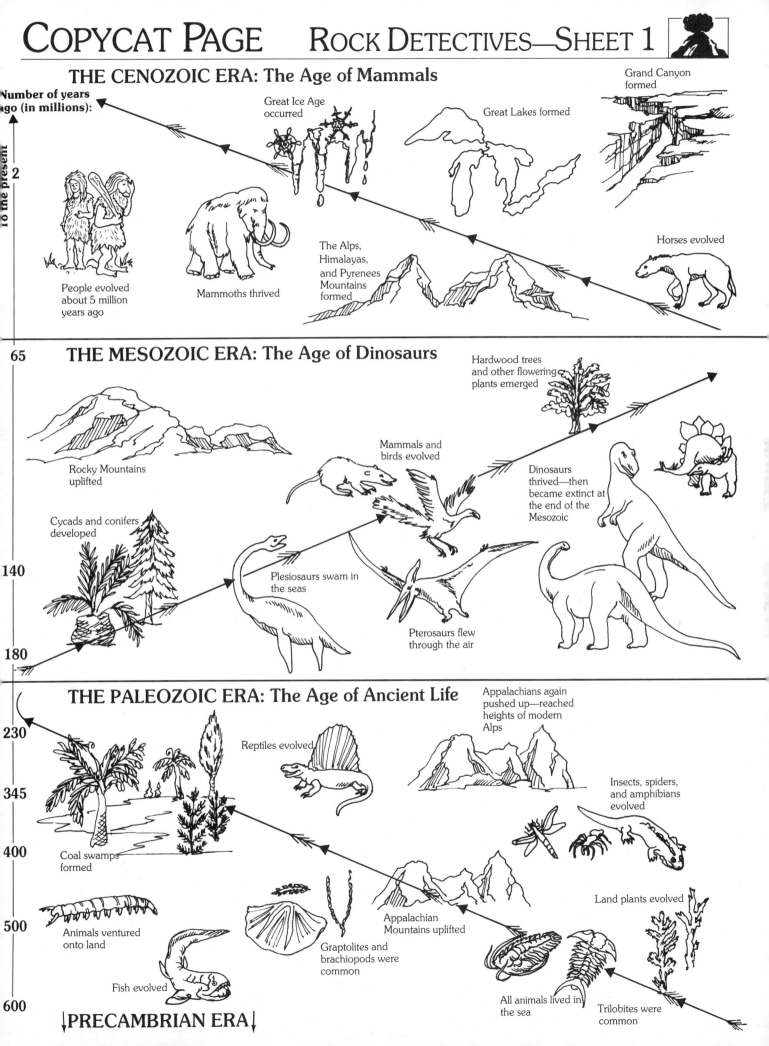

THE CENOZOIC ERA: The Age of Mammals

Number of years ago (in millions):

To the present

2

Great Ice Age occurred

Great Lakes formed

Grand Canyon formed

Horses evolved

The Alps, Himalayas, and Pyrenees Mountains formed

Mammoths thrived

People evolved about 5 million years ago

THE MESOZOIC ERA: The Age of Dinosaurs

65

Hardwood trees and other flowering plants emerged

Rocky Mountains uplifted

Cycads and conifers developed

Mammals and birds evolved

Dinosaurs thrived—then became extinct at the end of the Mesozoic

140

Plesiosaurs swam in the seas

Pterosaurs flew through the air

180

THE PALEOZOIC ERA: The Age of Ancient Life

Appalachians again pushed up—reached heights of modern Alps

230

Reptiles evolved

Insects, spiders, and amphibians evolved

345

400

Coal swamps formed

Appalachian Mountains uplifted

Land plants evolved

500

Animals ventured onto land

Graptolites and brachiopods were common

Fish evolved

All animals lived in the sea

Trilobites were common

600

↓ PRECAMBRIAN ERA ↓

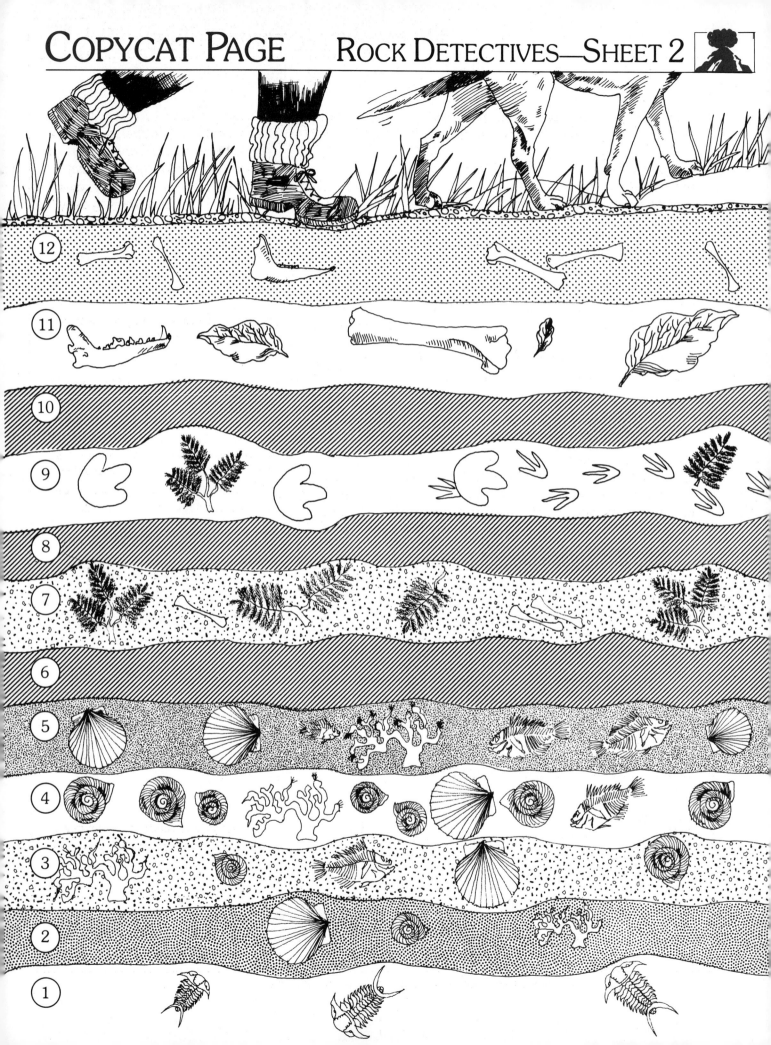

1. Gamlonia trees, a type of flowering plant, developed near the end of the Mesozoic Era.

2. The largest dinosaurs—some of which may have weighed as much as 80 tons (72 t)—were vegetarians. The largest meat-eating dinosaurs weighed much less—up to 10 tons (9 t).

3. Fossils form best in areas where a lot of fine sediment builds up. For example, many fossils form in shallow ocean areas near the mouths of rivers. That's because a lot of sediment can wash into these areas.

4. "Fakium" is a radioisotope with a half life of 300 million years. It breaks down into "hokium."

5. Layers 6, 8, and 10 are made up of igneous rock.

6. Rock that forms when magma or lava cools and hardens usually doesn't contain fossils. Any animals or plants that are covered by this molten rock usually burn up from the high temperatures.

7. In the mountains, wind, rain, and other factors are constantly at work, eroding the landscape and keeping sediment from accumulating.

8. Many of the world's landmasses were once joined, but have since drifted apart as crustal plates have shifted. For example, about 200 million years ago, all the world's landmasses were joined into one giant landmass which we now call Pangaea. Since Pangaea split apart, landmasses have continued to move apart, join together, and move apart again.

9. Dinosaurs became extinct about 65 million years ago.

10.  This plant grew in swamps near the end of the Paleozoic Era.

11. This footprint was made by an ostrich-sized, carnivorous dinosaur.

12. By studying fossils of this animal, paleontologists have discovered some of the ways it was adapted to its habitat. For example, they think that the hundreds of tiny claws on the animal's undersides helped it cling to rocks and kept it from washing away in the powerful surf. And the animal's tough shell seemed to be especially thick—an adaptation, paleontologists think, that protected it from marine predators and kept too much salt from entering its body.

13. This fossil jawbone belonged to a large, carnivorous animal.

14. **TOP VIEW (clockwise)** **BOTTOM VIEW** These snails lived in most of the world's oceans over a period of hundreds of millions of years. Paleontologists have discovered that in warm, tropical waters, there were more snails with shells which, when viewed from the top, spiraled in a clockwise direction. But in cool or cold waters, there were more snails with shells that spiraled in a counter-clockwise direction when viewed from the top.

15. Through the years, this sea plant gradually evolved spines. It grew in shallow seas.

16. This scallop-like fossil is never found in sediment less than 450 million years old.

17. This fossil jawbone belonged to a large animal.

18. This footprint was made by a dinosaur that weighed about 80 tons (72 t).

19.  This fish was abundant in shallow seas. It grazed on marine vegetation.

PEOPLE AND GEOLOGY

If you look at human culture and society from a geological point of view, it's easy to see just how firmly rooted in rock we've always been. First, for example, there was the Stone Age—that period in human development when people carved simple stone tools and weapons. Later, in the Bronze and Iron Ages, people started forging their implements out of metals dug from the Earth's rocky crust. The more sophisticated society and technology became, the more people relied on geologic resources.

These days our "rock foundation" is broader than ever. We use all kinds of minerals to make everything from forks to cars to computers—the tools of a modern world. And we fuel most of our activities with energy mined or pumped from the rocks beneath us. You could say, then, that the Earth's crust supports our entire civilization—in more ways than one.

SHAPED FROM STONE

Take a look around. Chances are you're surrounded by rocks and minerals in disguise: the foundation of your house, the glass in your windows, the wiring in your appliances, any gold or silver jewelry you might have. All of these things and many others once lay buried inside the Earth, in forms completely different from the ones technology has molded them into.

Extraordinary Elements: Some of the treasures we get from the Earth are the elements called metals. A long list of traits characterizes metals, such as the ability to conduct heat and electricity, a natural shine, the ability to be hammered into shapes (malleability), and a high density. Not all metals have all of these characteristics, though. Sodium, for example, is so light that it floats in water. And calcium isn't at all malleable (it's too brittle). But all metals have some combination of metallic traits.

A Spotty Distribution: There are dozens of different kinds of metals in the Earth's crust, but they usually aren't very abundant in any one place. Some metals (gold and silver, for example) are occasionally found in thick, pure veins. But usually these metals occur as tiny flakes within a rock. Other metals, such as iron, are almost always combined in a rock with other elements. But if a metal in a particular location is abundant enough to be mined for profit, it's known as an *ore.*

Mining and Refining: Before any metal can be transformed into something people can use, the rock it's contained within must first be *mined* (dug from the Earth). Next the metal itself must be *refined,* or extracted from the rock.

For some metals, the refining process can be expensive—in terms of both capital and energy. It can also be very complicated. Aluminum, for example, is the most abundant metallic element in the world. But it never occurs in a pure form. It's almost always bonded to several other elements, so it must be put through a very energy-intensive separation process. That's one reason that aluminum recycling is being encouraged more and more these days. (For more about aluminum and aluminum recycling, see "All About Aluminum" on page 64.)

Buried Treasures: It would be almost impossible for most of us to get through a day without using minerals. Here's a look at a few of the ways we use these natural resources every day:

- **An All-Purpose Mineral**—In some cultures, the mineral we call salt has been considered every bit as valuable as gold. This widespread mineral isn't just a flavoring for food. It's also used to make chemicals, medicines, and other products. Oil refineries and sewage treatment plants use salt too.
- **Getting the Lead Out**—The "lead" in pencils is another product of the Earth's crust. (It isn't really lead, though. It's graphite, a soft mineral once mistaken for its metallic namesake.) Graphite's softness makes it ideal for writing on paper.
- **Mineral Meltdown**—Every time you look out the window, you're gazing through minerals that have been melted together and quickly cooled into glass. The most important ingredient in glass is quartz sand that has been collected from beaches, desert sand dunes, or quartz sandstone.
- **Colors from the Earth**—The crust we stand on is a rainbow of hidden colors. Take iron, for example. It may not look very colorful in its pure form (which is usually dark), but when it's mixed with certain elements, bright reds, yellows, and oranges are formed. These and other elements and minerals often give paints their colors.
- **Beyond Beauty**—Some gemstones are more than beautiful—they're downright functional. Diamonds, for example, are the hardest naturally occurring substance in the world. They can cut or grind almost anything. This trait makes them valuable in the manufacturing of parts for cars, airplanes, and machines.

EARTH'S ENERGY

Minerals aren't the only valuables stored in the Earth's crust. There's also energy, mostly in the form of oil, natural gas, and coal. Together, all three *fossil fuels* (they're called "fossil" because they formed from the remains of ancient organisms) account for more than 90 percent of all the energy people use today.

"Black Gold": It's easy to see how oil got its nickname. This liquid fuel literally keeps the industrialized nations of the world running. It powers our cars, trucks, trains, and airplanes when it's converted into gasoline, diesel fuel, and jet fuel, and it's an integral part of the manufacturing of plastics, fertilizers, drugs, detergents, and many other products. Oil is also the main source of power for many factories, and it produces heat and/or electricity in some people's homes.

What's the original source of this "wonder fuel"? Countless billions of tiny marine organisms, according to most geologists. These plants and animals have lived and died in the Earth's seas for millions of years, adding their remains to the seafloor little by little. And from time to time certain "oil-producing" conditions have existed. Sometimes, for example, the sea organisms' remains have been buried before they could decompose. The layers the organisms were embedded in have gradually become compressed into rock. And the organisms themselves have slowly turned into the thick, dark liquid called crude oil. Today we pump the crude oil from its "reservoirs": tiny pore spaces within the rocky layers.

Ancient Sea Organisms Strike Again: Where there's oil, there's often natural gas. (Oil and natural gas aren't always associated, though—each can be found independently of the other.) Like oil, natural gas was "created" by ancient sea organisms that were partially decomposed and subjected to pressure and heat.

(continued next page)

The reason oil ended up as a liquid and natural gas ended up as a gas has to do with the intensity of the Earth's heat: At very high temperatures, natural gas forms and at lower temperatures oil forms.

Natural gas is used in many of the same ways oil is: It provides heat for homeowners and energy for industries, and it's important in the manufacturing of drugs, plastics, and other products. It's also used in certain ways that oil isn't, such as for cooking and air conditioning.

Swamp Plants on the Job: For a hundred years or so before the early 1900s, coal was the number one fuel in many parts of the world. It fueled the steam engines that powered the Industrial Revolution—and the nations that lacked an abundant supply of the hard, black substance were soon left behind.

Today coal is still an important fuel. (It may become more and more important in the next couple of decades, too, as oil and natural gas reserves dwindle.) Currently coal is used much more than any other fuel to drive the steam turbines of the electric power industry. And it's the only source of *coke*—a material that's crucial in the manufacturing of steel.

Ancient land plants, rather than marine organisms, are the sources of coal. As these plants died and fell in prehistoric swamp forests, they were gradually buried by other organic matter and subjected to pressure and heat. The pressure and heat gradually transformed the organic material into coal.

Pollution Problems: By using fossil fuels in so many ways, we've created some serious problems. For example, the burning of fossil fuels has caused severe air pollution in many parts of the world. And in some areas the pollutants in the air have resulted in another problem: acid rain. Water pollution can result from fossil fuel use too. Oil spills from tankers and offshore oil rigs have devastated populations of fish, birds, and other wildlife, and runoff from coal strip mines has sometimes poisoned streams and rivers.

Some of the products we make with fossil fuels also have negative effects. Plastics, for example, often end up in landfills—many of which are already overflowing. Most plastics aren't biodegradable, which means they'll still be sitting in the ground thousands of years from now unless they're incinerated. But incineration isn't always a good alternative, since many plastic products release toxic fumes when burned.

Many scientists are concerned that another fossil fuel-related problem could have catastrophic effects in the future. The burning of fossil fuels, they say, could change the composition of the atmosphere and lead to an overall warming of the Earth's climate. And that could mean big troubles for many of the Earth's ecosystems.

We Can All Help: We've made some progress in dealing with these "side effects" of fossil fuel use. Strict air and water pollution laws have helped a lot. So have laws requiring that strip mines be *reclaimed,* or made to look much as they did before the area was mined. (Reclamation not only covers an eyesore—it also helps prevent erosion and poisonous runoff.) There's still a lot to be done, though, and there's plenty of room for citizens to get involved. Many people adopted a lot of good habits during the energy crunch of the '70s, such as keeping thermostats turned down and joining car pools. And there's no reason to let these conservation habits slide. Industrialized nations are burning more and more fossil fuels these days—and supplies won't last forever. (At the rate we're going, for example, the demand for oil could surpass the supply before the year 2100.) Try "All About Aluminum" on page 64 to help your kids learn more about conserving one of the resources we get from the Earth's crust.

Geoscavenge

Take part in a geology scavenger hunt.

Objective:
Name several things made from minerals, petroleum, or coal.

Ages:
Primary, Intermediate, and Advanced

Materials:
- *copies of the scavenger hunt list provided in the activity*
- *aluminum can*
- *aluminum foil*
- *pencil*
- *metal toy car*
- *mirror*
- *drinking glass*
- *metal scissors*
- *metal spoon or table knife*
- *book*
- *wooden spoon*
- *paper*
- *plant*
- *table*
- *pencils*
- *paper bags*
- *magazines*
- *glue (optional)*
- *construction paper (optional)*

Subject:
Science

I n this activity your kids can take part in a scavenger hunt to learn about the variety of products that come from rocks, minerals, and other resources in the Earth's crust. You can choose between a version for younger kids (Part 1: What Comes from Rocks) and one for older kids (Part 2: A Rock and Mineral Hunt).

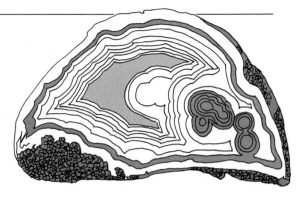

PART 1: WHAT COMES FROM ROCKS

Before the kids arrive, place these materials on a table: aluminum can, aluminum foil, a metal spoon or table knife, a pencil, a metal toy car, a mirror, a drinking glass, a pair of metal scissors, a wooden spoon, a book, some paper, and a plant. You can set up one table for the whole group or place identical sets of items on several tables for smaller groups of kids. Then cover the items or move the tables so the kids can't see them.

Begin by asking the kids if they can name a way that people use rocks. Ask them if anyone lives in a house made of stone or brick. See if they can name other familiar things that are made with rocks. (other buildings, roads, sidewalks, statues, and so on)

Now ask if anyone knows what rocks are made of. Explain that all rocks are made up of one or more minerals. For example, granite is a common rock that is usually made up of the minerals quartz, feldspar, and mica. (See pages 17-18 for more about minerals.) Explain that people use many of the minerals that are found in rocks to make a variety of products. For example, we use the quartz in sandstone to make glass and we use the copper in copper ore to make pennies.

Now uncover or bring out the table. Ask the kids which of the items on the table are mineral products. As a group, have them separate the items into those things that come from minerals and those things that are not mineral products. (All are mineral products except the book, paper, plant, and wooden spoon. See the

section called "Mineral Products" [below] to find out which minerals are used to make each item.)

Now tell the kids that you'll be reading clues that describe the things on the table that are mineral products. After you read a clue, tell them to "hunt" for the object that fits.

Clues:
- something that's easy to crumple (foil)
- something that soda comes in (can)
- something you write with (pencil)
- something you play with (metal toy car)
- something you can see yourself in (mirror)
- something you might drink milk from (drinking glass)
- something you cut paper with (metal scissors)
- something you eat ice cream with (metal spoon)

You can also practice some classification skills with the kids. Have them divide the mineral products into things found at a dinner table, things they use at school, heavy and light items, and so on. As a follow-up, you may want to read the kids "The Magic of Rocks," *Ranger Rick,* June 1984, pp 4-11.

Mineral products: foil (aluminum, which is made from bauxite), soda can (aluminum), metal toy car (aluminum and/or steel, which is made from iron), pencil "lead" (graphite), drinking glass and mirror (glass made from the quartz in sand or sandstone), metal scissors (steel), metal spoon (steel or aluminum)

(continued next page)

BRANCHING OUT: CREATING COLLAGES

Have your kids make geology collages. Pass out magazines and tell the kids to cut out pictures that are related in some way to geology. For example, they could include pictures of landforms such as mountains and valleys, geological events such as earthquakes or volcanoes, or products such as soda cans or diamond rings.

Then pass out construction paper and glue and have the kids glue down their cut-out pictures.

PART 2: A ROCK AND MINERAL HUNT

SCAVENGER HUNT LIST

Find these things:
1. stone building
2. car, truck, or airplane
3. plastic bag you can store food in
4. toothpaste
5. tombstone made of rock
6. pencil
7. window
8. nylon stocking
9. paper clip
10. dishwashing detergent
11. shoe polish
12. faucet
13. cement
14. aluminum can
15. plastic eyeglass frames
16. clock or watch
17. scissors
18. plastic garbage bag
19. plastic fork or spoon
20. pottery
21. jewelry
22. chalk
23. paint
24. petroleum jelly
25. lipstick

First make copies of the scavenger hunt list in the margin. (You'll need one copy for every two or three kids.) Then divide the group into teams of two or three and give each team a copy of the list of items, a paper bag, and some pencils. Tell the kids that the object of the hunt is to try to find everything on the list. Explain that they should put items that can be collected into their paper bags. But if they see an object that can't be collected (a car, for example), they can just check it on their lists. They can also go through magazines and cut out pictures of the clues they can't collect or find. (You may want to set a time limit and define safe boundaries for the scavenger hunt before the kids begin.)

The team that finds the most items within the time limit wins.

When the hunt is over, gather the teams together and go over the kids' "finds." Tell the kids to circle the things on the list that are made from minerals, rocks, petroleum, or coal—all natural substances found in the Earth's crust. (You may want to review the definition of a rock and a mineral, and explain the origins of petroleum and coal. See pages 17-19 and 58-60.)

Then, using the information below, tell the kids which resource each object is made from. They might be surprised to find that *all* the objects on the list were made from rocks, minerals, petroleum, or coal.

PETROLEUM PRODUCTS
plastic food bag
nylon stocking
plastic eyeglass frames
plastic garbage bag
petroleum jelly
plastic fork or spoon
lipstick

COAL PRODUCT
shoe polish

MINERAL PRODUCTS
pottery
window (most glass is made from sand, which is mostly quartz)
dishwashing detergent
toothpaste
chalk
pencil "lead"
clock or watch

scissors
faucet
jewelry (some costume jewelry is made with plastic)
paint (different metal oxides give paints their colors)
paper clip
aluminum can
car, truck, airplane

ROCK PRODUCTS
cement
stone building
tombstone

Geology Chronology

Write newspaper articles about geological events.

Objective:
Describe several historical events related to geology.

Ages:
Intermediate and Advanced

Materials:
- *paper*
- *pencils*
- *newsprint*
- *black pens or markers*
- *reference books*
- *chalkboard or easel paper*
- *current news article*
- *newspapers and magazines (optional)*
- *bulletin board (optional)*
- *construction paper (optional)*

Subjects:
Science and Language Arts

hroughout human history, geological happenings such as the discovery of gold in California or the 1980 eruption of Mount St. Helens have always been "big news." In this activity your kids can learn about these and other dramatic geological events of the past by writing their own newspaper articles.

On the day of the activity, bring in a short geology-related newspaper article. Also copy the list of events below on the chalkboard or piece of easel paper. Read the newspaper article to the kids and then, as a group, list some of the facts they learned from the article on the chalkboard or another piece of easel paper. Show how the facts answer the five "Ws": who, what, where, when, and why. Explain that many news writers often try to answer these questions to make sure the readers get a complete account of a news event.

Next show the kids the list of geological events you copied earlier. Tell the kids that some of these events happened long ago, but others have occurred very recently. Explain that each person will get to choose one of the events and write a newspaper article about it, pretending to be a reporter living at the time the event occurred. You may want to read the example below to get them started. (Note: The account by Pliny in the following sample is not a real quote.)

VESUVIUS BLOWS ITS TOP!

Naples, Aug. 25, AD 79: Mt. Vesuvius, a volcano once thought to be extinct, erupted yesterday. Pliny the Elder, an eyewitness to the disaster, described the scene in a letter he wrote shortly before he died of a heart attack during the eruption:

"Tons of burning ash are falling upon the nearby city of Pompeii. Burning hot gases from the eruption are filling the air. We can hardly breathe because of the ash and heat."

Other reports indicate that thousands of people choked on the gases and were buried by ash. Herculaneum, another city near the volcano, was covered with at least 60 feet of mud. Both cities were completely destroyed, and only a few people escaped.

The volcano appears to have stopped erupting. But people are warned to stay away from the area. Many fear that the volcano could erupt again at any time.

GEOLOGICAL EVENTS

- Alaska earthquake (1964)
- Discovery of Mid-Atlantic Ridge (1872)
- El Chichon erupts (1982, Mexico)
- Eldfell erupts on the island of Heimaey (1973, Iceland)
- Gold rush in the North American West (1849)
- Guatemala City earthquake (1986)
- Island of Surtsey forms in the Atlantic Ocean (1963)
- Krakatoa erupts (1883)
- Lisbon earthquake (1755, Portugal)
- Lunar rock samples brought back by Apollo 11 astronauts (1969)
- Mexico City earthquake (1985)
- Mt. Pelee erupts (1902, West Indies)
- Mount St. Helens erupts (1980)
- New Madrid, Missouri earthquakes (1811-12)
- Oil crisis in the 1970s
- San Francisco earthquake (1906)
- Spanish search for gold in South America (1553)
- Tokyo earthquake (1923)
- Underwater hot springs discovered near the Galapagos Islands (1977)

Pass out paper and pencils and give the kids research time to put together rough drafts of their articles. Remind the kids to write their articles as if they were living at the time the event occurred, and to try to answer the five "Ws." Then have the kids copy their articles on newsprint with black pens or markers, making sure to include the name of the newspaper, the date, and the title of the article. When everyone is finished, ask a few volunteers to read their articles to the group.

As a follow-up to the activity, have the kids check newspapers and magazines each day for articles related to geology. They can keep a group journal or make a geology bulletin board to display the articles.

(continued next page)

Make geology come alive by turning your kids into TV news reporters! Divide the group into news teams of three or four. Have the kids choose one or two of the news articles they wrote to present in the newscast. The teams can decide who will be the anchor person, the on-the-scene reporter, and the eyewitnesses. They can also illustrate their stories on construction paper. Have each team take a turn at being "on the air" in front of the rest of the group.

All About Aluminum

Learn how aluminum is made and recycled. Take part in a recycling drive in your community.

Objectives:
Name several ways aluminum is used. Describe two steps in the aluminum-making process. Explain how aluminum and other mineral resources can be conserved.

Ages:
Advanced

Materials:
- *copies of page 67*
- *copy of the math problems on page 65*
- *chalkboard or easel paper*
- *poster paper*
- *paper*
- *pencils*
- *markers, crayons, or poster paints*

Subjects:
Science and Math

Lightweight, strong, and rust-resistant—aluminum is the second most popular metal in the world. (Only iron is used more.) In this two-part activity your kids can learn more about how aluminum is mined and then take part in the effort to recycle it.

First ask the kids to name as many things as they can think of that have aluminum in them and list their answers on a chalkboard or piece of easel paper. (You may want to add some of the aluminum products from the following list.)

ALUMINUM IN 'EM

air conditioners	lawn chairs
airplanes	paint
aluminum foil	refrigerators
baseball bats	road signs
beverage cans	ships
cars	siding for buildings
cookware	spacecraft
doors	toys
electrical wires	trains
food cans	trucks
gutters	window frames
hand tools	
heat-resistant suits for firefighters	

Next explain that aluminum is made from an ore called *bauxite*. (An ore is a mineral or rock in the Earth's crust that contains enough metal to make it profitable to mine.) Then pass out a copy of page 67 to everyone. The chart on the left shows the major steps in the aluminum-making process. (To make it easier for the kids, we left out a few of the steps and simplified others.) The other chart shows the steps in the aluminum recycling process.

Starting with the first chart, have the kids follow along as you use the following information to explain each step.

#1: Most bauxite is mined in open pits. First bulldozers clear away trees, rocks, and topsoil. Then the ore is loosened with explosives, loaded into trucks, and taken to processing plants or storage areas.
#2: At processing plants, the bauxite is crushed into small particles and sprayed with water to remove dirt, sand, and other waste. Then it's heated to remove any remaining water.
#3: The crushed and washed bauxite is transported to a refinery. (To *refine* means to extract a mineral from rock.) Using a series of chemical reactions, the bauxite is refined into *alumina*. Alumina is a fine white powder that can vary in consistency from that of talcum powder to that of granulated sugar.
#4: Alumina is taken to a smelter (also called a reduction plant). It is placed in a huge "pot" where oxygen is removed. The molten aluminum collects in the bottom of the pot and is siphoned into a holding tank. (Step 4 uses a lot of electricity.)
#5: The molten aluminum is transported to a cast house, usually located near the smelter. Here other metals may be added to the molten aluminum to make it stronger. The aluminum is then poured into molds and cooled to form *ingots*. These ingots can be in the shape of long, thin cylinders, huge sheets, or thick squares.
#6: The aluminum ingots may be remelted, hammered, squeezed, or rolled into a variety of products.

New aluminum made from bauxite is called *primary* aluminum. Point out to the kids that about one-fourth of all the aluminum in the world is made in the United States. But all the bauxite used to make aluminum is imported into the United States from other countries. A large amount of alumina is also imported from outside the U.S. (There are no significant deposits of bauxite in the United States, although there are reserves of other ores from which alumina can be refined. The reason these reserves are not mined is that it's cheaper to import bauxite from other countries.)

Next have the kids look at the chart that shows the steps in aluminum recycling. Here is a brief explanation of each step:

#1: Beverage cans, car parts, appliances, and other used aluminum products are collected at recycling centers and scrap dealers. The aluminum is crushed into bales so it can be transported more easily.
#2: The used aluminum is melted. This takes much less electricity than the amount needed to turn alumina into aluminum.
#3: The molten aluminum is poured into molds.
#4: This *secondary* aluminum, or aluminum made from melted-down scrap, can be reshaped into many products.

Ask the kids if they can name some of the things that can be saved by recycling. (bauxite, land that's otherwise destroyed by mining, money to buy and transport bauxite, electricity) Then tell them that, although a lot of progress has been made, we still have a long way to go in the effort to recycle aluminum. In 1985, only half of the 65 billion aluminum cans made in the United States were recycled. (Many of the unrecycled cans ended up as litter on highways and in other places.) And millions of pounds of aluminum in the form of appliances, car parts, and other products are still being dumped in landfills instead of being reused.

Wind up this part of the activity by having the kids discuss the following questions.

- What are some reasons that more people don't recycle? (people may think it's inconvenient to collect aluminum products and transport them to recycling centers; people may not know where to take products)
- What are some pros and cons of recycling? (Pros—save energy, mineral resources, money; reduce litter; reduce the amount of land used for landfills; receive money for cans taken to recycling centers. Cons—sometimes inconvenient to recycle; burning paints and other toxic materials in the recycling process can cause air pollution if proper filters aren't used to trap toxic fumes.)
- What are some ways to encourage recycling? (pay for materials that can be recycled; educate people about the benefits of recycling; make it more convenient to recycle; hold recycling drives; work to establish recycling laws)

Electricity Used by Appliances in a Year (average kilowatt hours)

Clock	17 kwh
Hair dryer	25 kwh
Toaster	39 kwh
Vacuum cleaner	46 kwh
Radio	86 kwh
Washing machine	103 kwh
Coffeemaker	140 kwh
Dishwasher	165 kwh
Window fan	170 kwh
Color television	320 kwh
Range with oven	626 kwh
Clothes dryer	993 kwh
Freezer (with automatic defrost)	1820 kwh

PART 2: RECYCLING AND MATH

Demonstrate some of the benefits of aluminum recycling by solving the following math problems. Tell the kids to suppose that each person in your group used and saved one aluminum can a day. Then copy the following problems on a chalkboard or piece of easel paper and give the kids time to work on them. Tell them to solve the problems using a 30-day month. Also copy the list of electrical energy requirements on the left. (The answers on the next page are for a group of 25 kids.)

1. How many aluminum cans would your group have collected at the end of a week? At the end of a month?

2. 27 aluminum cans weigh one pound (.45 kg). How many pounds of aluminum could you collect in a month?

3. Recycling one pound of aluminum saves four pounds (1.8 kg) of bauxite. How many pounds of bauxite could you save by recycling the cans saved in a month?

4. Recycling one pound of aluminum saves about 7.6 kilowatt hours of electricity. How much electricity could you save by recycling the cans saved in a month? (Have the kids look at the list of electrical appliance energy requirements to help them understand the amount of electricity that could be saved. For example, saving 165 kwh by recycling aluminum could power a dishwasher for a year.)

5. If you receive 20¢ for each pound of aluminum brought to a recycling center, how much money could you make from the cans saved in a month?

Note: This is an average price per pound of aluminum. It will vary depending on your location and the current market price for aluminum.

(continued next page)

Answers to Sample Problems

1. 25 cans/day × 7 days/week = 175 cans/week
   25 cans/day × 30 days/month = 750 cans/month
2. 750 cans ÷ 27 cans/pound = 28 lbs (rounded off)
3. 28 lbs × 4 lbs bauxite/1 lb aluminum = 112 lbs of bauxite
4. 28 lbs × 7.6 kwh/1 lb aluminum = 213 kwh (about the amount of electricity needed to power two washing machines for a year)
5. 28 lbs × 20¢/1 lb aluminum = $5.60

BRANCHING OUT: COMMUNITY INVOLVEMENT

Here are some ways to get your group, as well as the whole community, involved in recycling.

- Start a recycling drive. (See "How to Organize a Recycling Drive" below.)
- Take the kids on a litter pick-up walk to clean up the area—and add some extra pounds of glass and aluminum to the recycling drive. (You may want to tell the kids that scientists think it might take hundreds of years for an aluminum can to decompose. You can also talk about the problems associated with burying trash in landfills. Explain that toxic runoff from landfills is often a very serious problem. Also, many areas are running out of places to put their trash.)
- Many kids may not realize that plastics can be recycled too. And because plastic is made from petroleum, another valuable mineral resource, its conservation is especially important. (Plastics are also a big part of the problem of overflowing landfills. [Most plastics aren't biodegradable.] And more and more products are being packaged in plastics.)
- Support recycling laws. Some areas have already passed laws that encourage recycling. Contact conservation organizations in your area for more information about recycling laws.

HOW TO ORGANIZE A RECYCLING DRIVE

1. Decide what you want to recycle. For example, you can collect newspapers, glass, plastic, and/or aluminum. Also decide on a time frame for the drive—whether it will last for one day or be held one day each month for a few months.
2. Contact a recycling collector in your area at least six to seven weeks before the drive is held. (Check the Yellow Pages under "recycling." You can also call 1-800-228-2525 from anywhere in the United States to find the aluminum recycling center closest to you.) Be sure the collector agrees to accept the materials you've decided to collect. And check on any rules the collector may have. For example, most glass and can collectors prefer getting clean containers. Also, many glass collectors require that you remove metal caps and rings and separate the glass by color.
3. Arrange for a place, such as an empty schoolroom or someone's garage, to store the collected materials. This is important if you're holding the drive over a few months or can't transport the materials to the recycling center immediately.
4. Choose a convenient location for the drive, such as a school, shopping area, or recreation center. The area should have easy access and be clearly visible from the road. Check with the proper authorities for permission to use the area.
5. Line up transportation to get materials from the storage or collection area to the recycling center.
6. Publicize the drive. Make posters and/or fliers to tell people what you are collecting. Include the date, time, and location of the drive. You may want to include some of the information given in this activity's discussion and in the math problems to convince people that recycling is important. You can also contact local newspapers and radio stations to see if they'll advertise the drive.
7. Think about how your group can spend the money it makes. You could use it to fund your club, donate it to a local wildlife center or other organization, or finance a long-term recycling program.

COPYCAT PAGE

ALL ABOUT ALUMINUM

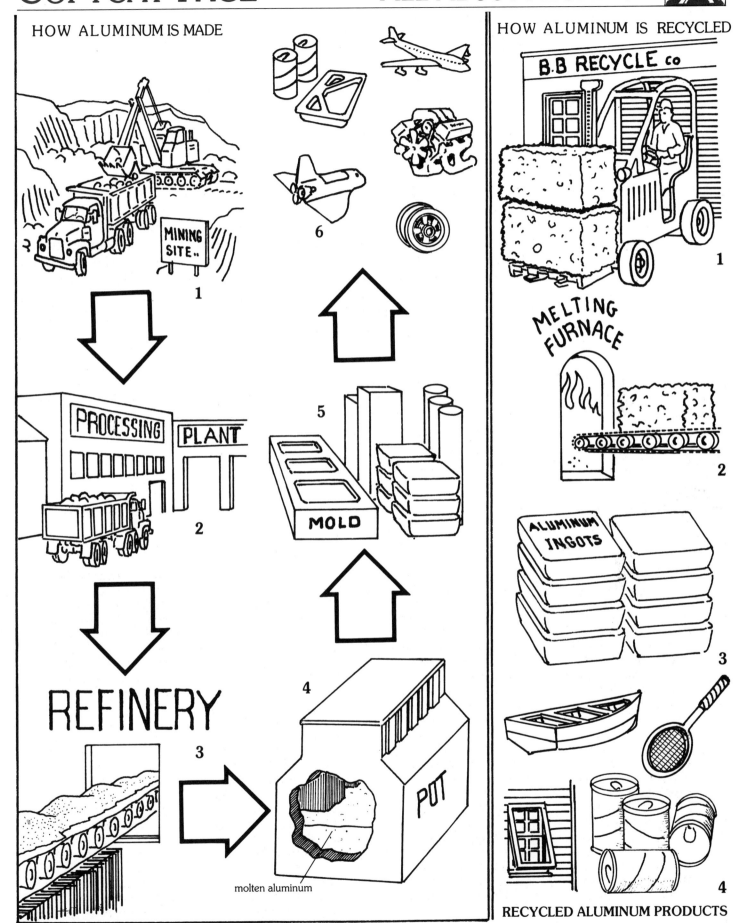

HOW ALUMINUM IS MADE

MINING SITE 1

PROCESSING PLANT 2

REFINERY 3

molten aluminum

POT 4

MOLD 5

6

HOW ALUMINUM IS RECYCLED

B.B RECYCLE CO 1

MELTING FURNACE 2

ALUMINUM INGOTS 3

RECYCLED ALUMINUM PRODUCTS 4

APPENDIX— Bibliography

(Note: A ♟ at the end of a listing indicates that a book is a good source of geology pictures.)

GENERAL REFERENCE BOOKS

Crystals and Crystal Growing by Alan Holden and Phylis Morrison (MIT, 1982)

Exploring Our Living Planet by Robert D. Ballard (National Geographic Society, 1983) ♟

Fossils: The Key to the Past by Richard Fortey (Van Nostrand Reinhold, 1982) ♟

Giants from the Past (National Geographic Society, 1983)

The Making of a Continent by Ron Redfern (American Geological Institute, 1983) ♟

Nature on the Rampage (National Geographic Society, 1986) ♟

Our Continent: A Natural History of North America (National Geographic Society, 1976)

Planet Earth is a series including *Continents in Collision, Earthquake, Gemstones, Glacier, Ice Ages,* and *Volcano.* (Time-Life, 1982) ♟

FIELD GUIDES

Audubon Society Field Guide to North American Rocks and Minerals by Charles W. Chesterman (Knopf, 1978) ♟

Fossil Collector's Handbook: A Paleontology Field Guide by James Reid Macdonald (Prentice-Hall, 1983)

Fossils by Frank H.T. Rhodes (Golden, 1962) ♟

Fossils in Colour by J.F. Kirkaldy (Blandford, 1984) ♟

Guide to Rocks and Minerals edited by Martin Prinz et al. (Simon & Schuster, 1978) ♟

Minerals and Rocks by J.F. Kirkaldy (Blandford, 1984)

Rocks and Minerals by Pat Bell and David Wright (Macmillan, 1985) ♟

Rocks and Minerals by Charles A. Sorrell (Golden, 1973) ♟

CHILDREN'S BOOKS

Album of Rocks and Minerals by Tom McGowen (Rand McNally, 1981). Intermediate and Advanced ♟

Collecting Small Fossils by Lois J. Hussey and Catherine Pessino (Crowell, 1970). Intermediate and Advanced

Disastrous Volcanoes by Melvin Berger (Franklin Watts, 1981). Intermediate

Discovering Fossils by Wendy Rydell (Troll, 1984). Primary and Intermediate

The Earth by Keith Lye (Silver Burdett Color Library, Macmillan, 1980). Advanced ♟

Earth, Sea and Sky: An Illustrated Encyclopedia (Arco, 1984). Intermediate and Advanced ♟

Geology by Dougal Dixon (Aladdin, 1982). Intermediate and Advanced

Glaciers by D.V. Georges (Childrens Press, 1986). Primary ♟

Glaciers by Wendell V. Tangborn (Crowell, 1988). Primary ♟

Glaciers and Ice Sheets by Gordon De Q. Robin (Bookwright, 1984). Intermediate ♟

The How and Why Wonder Book of Fossils by John Burton (Grosset & Dunlap, 1976). Intermediate

How to Dig a Hole to the Other Side of the World by Faith McNulty (Harper & Row, 1979). Primary

Icebergs by Roma Gans (Crowell, 1987). Primary

If You Are a Hunter of Fossils by Byrd Baylor and Peter Parnall (Scribners, 1980). Primary

Inside the Earth by Alan Davis (Grosset & Dunlap, 1972). Advanced

Land Masses: Fun, Facts, and Activities by Caroline Arnold (Watts, 1985). Primary and Intermediate

Man and Materials is a series of six books edited by Ian Ridpath. Titles include *Coal, Gas, Minerals, Oil, Plastics,* and *Stone.* (Addison Wesley, 1975). Intermediate

The Mount St. Helens Disaster: What We've Learned by Thomas G. and Virginia L. Aylesworth (Watts, 1983). Advanced ♟

Mountains by Martyn Bramwell (Earth Science Library, Franklin Watts, 1986). Advanced ♟

Mountains and Earth Movements by Ian Bain (Bookwright, 1984). Intermediate

Nature's World of Wonders (National Geographic Society, 1983). Advanced ♟

Our Violent Earth (National Geographic Society, 1982). Advanced ♟

Planet Earth by Martyn Bramwell (Earth Science Library, Franklin Watts, 1987). Advanced

Rock Collecting by Roma Gans (Crowell, 1984). Primary and Intermediate

The Rock Hound's Book by Seymour Simon (Viking, 1973). Advanced

Rockhound Trails by Jean Bartenback (Atheneum, 1977). Intermediate

Rocks and Minerals by Dr. R.F. Symes and the staff of the Natural History Museum/London (Knopf, 1988). Advanced ♟

The Story of Geology by Jerome Wyckoff (Golden, 1976). Advanced ♟

Understanding and Collecting Rocks and Fossils by Martyn Bramwell (Usborne, 1983). Advanced

Volcano: The Eruption and Healing of Mount St. Helens by Patricia Lauber (Bradbury, 1980). Intermediate

Volcanoes by David Lambert (Watts, 1985). Intermediate and Advanced ♟

Volcanoes by Seymour Simon (Morrow, 1988). Primary ♟

Volcanoes and Earthquakes by Terry Jennings (Marshall Cavendish, 1989). Advanced ♟

Volcanoes in Our Solar System by G. Jeffrey Taylor (Dodd Mead, 1983). Advanced

What Can She Be? A Geologist by Gloria Goldreich and Esther Goldreich (Lothrop, 1978). Primary and Intermediate

When You Find a Rock by Barrie Klaits (Macmillan, 1976). Intermediate

The Work of the Wind by David Lambert (Bookwright, 1984). Intermediate ♟

FILMS, FILMSTRIPS, AND VIDEOS

Coronet Film & Video has many geology films for all ages. For more information write Coronet Film & Video, 108 Wilmot Rd., Deerfield, IL 60015.

The Earth Explored (Advanced) is a series of fourteen 28-minute geology videos from PBS VIDEO. For more information write PBS VIDEO, 1320 Braddock Pl., Alexandria, VA 22314.

Earth: The Restless Planet (Advanced) is available in film or video from Karol Media, 350 N. Pennsylvania Ave., Wilkes-Barre, PA 18773.

Encyclopaedia Britannica has films on many geology topics for all ages. For more information write Britannica Films and Video, 310 S. Michigan Ave., Chicago, IL 60604.

Introducing Geology (Intermediate and Advanced) is a set of six filmstrips with cassettes, teacher's guides, and ready-to-copy pages. For more information write Society for Visual Education, Dept. BJ, 1345 Diversey Pkwy., Chicago, IL 60614-1299.

National Geographic Society has several filmstrips with cassettes and teacher's guides for all ages. For more information write National Geographic Society, Educational Services, Dept. 90, Washington, DC 20036.

Booklets, Kits, Maps, and Posters

American Geological Institute has books and pamphlets on many geology topics, including *The Making of a Continent*, a companion volume to the PBS series of the same title. *Earth science*, a quarterly geology magazine for the general public, and "A Study in Time," a poster on geologic time periods, are also available. For more information write American Geological Institute, 4220 King St., Alexandria, VA 22302.

Massachusetts Audubon Society has reprints from the *Curious Naturalist* on geology topics including "Snow Geology" (Vol. II), "Pangaea—Drifting Continents" (Vol. X), and "Energy from the Earth" (Vol. XIV). "The Rock Cycle" and "Geologic Time" are charts that are also available. Write Massachusetts Audubon Society, Public Information Office, Great South Rd., Lincoln, MA 01773.

National Geographic Society has topographic and satellite image maps of the Grand Canyon, the United States, and the Americas. Write National Geographic Society, Educational Services, Dept. 90, Washington, DC 20036.

U.S. Geological Survey has many pamphlets, books, maps, lists of resources, and a teacher's packet, among other items. Many of these materials are free. For more information, write U.S. Geological Survey, Geologic Inquiries Group, 907 National Center, Reston, VA 22092.

U.S. Government Printing Office has a current subject bibliography on earth science publications (order #SB 160). Write to the U.S. Government Printing Office, Superintendent of Documents, Washington, DC 20402-9325.

Other Activity Sources

American Coal Foundation has activity booklets for grades K-6 and above, along with coal samples. For more information and an order form write American Coal Foundation, 1130 17th St. NW, Suite 220, Washington, DC 20036.

Earth Sciences and Rocks (Intermediate) is an activity guide available from British Columbia Teachers' Federation. For a catalog write B.C. Teachers' Federation, Lesson Aids Service, 2235 Burrard St., Vancouver, BC V6J 3H9.

Where To Get Rock And Mineral Samples

Carolina Biological Supply Company has rock and mineral samples, fossils, and other geology materials. For more information write Carolina Biological Supply Company, 2700 York Rd., Burlington, NC 27215.

Delta Education has rock and mineral samples, crystal-growing kits, charts, and guides. Write Delta Education, P.O. Box 915, Hudson, NH 03051.

Ward's Natural Science Establishment has rock and mineral samples, fossils, and many other materials. For more information write Ward's Natural Science Establishment, Inc., 5100 West Henrietta Rd., P.O. Box 92912, Rochester, NY 14692-9012.

Software

Earth: The Inside Story (Intermediate and Advanced) and **The Earth Through Time and Space** (Advanced) are available for Apple II. Each package offers colorful graphics, questions with a useful "help" feature, and the option to play a game along with the questions. Write Educational Activities, Inc., P.O. Box 392, Freeport, NY 11520.

Mineral Tests (Advanced) is available for Apple II. Program contains colorful graphics and a "help" section for learning the properties of minerals. Write Focus Media, Inc., 839 Stewart Ave., P.O. Box 865, Garden City, NY 11530.

Where To Get More Information

- college and university departments of geology
- museums
- nature centers
- rock and mineral clubs

Ranger Rick Geology Index

Ranger Rick, *published by the National Wildlife Federation, is a monthly nature magazine for elementary-age children.*

1997 UPDATE

TABLE OF CONTENTS

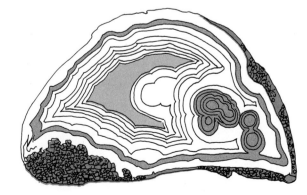

LIQUID ROCKS AND SOLID WATER: GEOLOGY OF THE UNIVERSE

by Jim Mack

Do you ever wonder why other planets look the way they do? Where did all those weird shapes on the surface of Mars come from? What forces could cause such huge craters on the moon? The answers to these questions about geology far out in space may be as close as your own feet. You could help unlock the secrets of the landscape on Mars by exploring the surface of Earth.

The Earth we walk on today has been shaped primarily by volcanoes and glaciers. Their boiling, churning, and crunching movements have molded our modern landscape and left clues about the geology of the universe. As we prepare to explore other planets, evidence from volcanoes and glaciers can provide us with valuable information about the geology of the universe. Take a look at the landscape here on Earth and see what you can discover.

Geology And Volcanoes

The deep center of the Earth is so hot that it is made of melted rock. Occasionally, this hot liquid rock, called *magma*, works its way to the surface when a volcano erupts. Scientists investigate volcanic eruptions like detectives, looking for evidence to help explain geology here on Earth and throughout the solar system.

You can be a geology sleuth, too. Our national park system preserves some of the nation's most fascinating volcanic sites for you and your family to explore. A list of parks and monuments at the end of this essay will help you plan trips to see giant craters, lava tubes, and maybe even a volcanic bomb! Read on and learn more about the clues that volcanic eruptions have left for today's geology detectives.

Clue #1: Shape

There are three basic volcano shapes. Each shape tells something about how the volcano was formed.

1. *Cinder Cone.* Cinder cones are formed by volcanic cinders that are thrown into the air during an eruption and then fall back down around the vent—the volcano opening. The heavier cinders usually fall closer to the vent and the lighter materials are thrown further away.

The tops of cinder cones are usually rounded, not pointed. They have a small bowl-shaped crater.

If you take a handful of sand and pour it out into a pile, you'll have an idea of how this type of volcano is shaped. Eruptions that create cinder cones are not very powerful explosions. There are many examples of cinder cones in the western United States.

2. *Shield Volcano.* When magma—the hot liquid rock from the earth's core—reaches the surface of the earth, it is called *lava.* A shield volcano is formed by layer after layer of lava flowing out of the volcano vent and then cooling. Shield volcanoes are found in Hawaii and Iceland, as well as other parts of the world. There is a shield volcano called Crater Lake Mountain in Lassen National Park, California.

A shield volcano is usually broad, with a low dome instead of steep sides.

Mauna Loa   349°E

Using what they knew about volcanoes on Earth, scientists were able to identify shield volcanoes in the Tharsis region of Mars from pictures sent to Earth by the Viking spacecraft.

3. *Composite Cone.* A composite cone is a combination of a cinder cone and a shield volcano. It is formed by alternating layers of lava flows and cinders. Composite cone volcanoes are often very striking. Examples are Mount Shasta in California, Mount Rainier in Washington, and the famous Mount Fuji in Japan.

Composite cones are formed by lava and cinders from a single vent. The base of the volcano is circular.

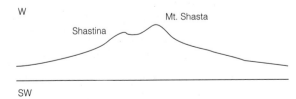

W

Shastina   Mt. Shasta

SW

Clue #2: Lava

Now let's get up close to examine some of the evidence from volcanoes. The next clue to look at is the lava. There are two types of lava.

1. *Aa Lava.* Aa (pronounced "ah-ah") lava has a rough and jagged surface. Its sharp edges can be very tough on shoes and unprotected hands. Aa lava is formed when the surface layer, or skin, of the lava solidifies and the underlying lava continues to flow. This makes the surface crumble and break up into a rough jumble of rock. These rough rocks are called *clinkers* because of the "clinking" sound they make as they break off from the front of the moving lava flow.

2. *Pahoehoe Lava.* Pahoehoe (pronounced "pah-hoy-hoy") is very different from aa lava. Its surface looks like a series of smooth ropes. Pahoehoe pours across the land like hot, thick fudge until it cools and forms its "ropy" texture.

Pahoehoe lava frequently forms *lava tubes*, which are like lava caves that form as the lava cools. The outer edge of the lava cools and solidifies, while the center remains liquid. As the volcanic eruption and the lava flow slow down, the liquid center drains out, leaving an empty tube. Lava tubes can be over a mile long.

Lava tubes have been identified on the slopes of Martian volcanoes, an important clue for scientists. On Earth, the Heppe cave in Lava Beds National Monument in California is one excellent example of a lava tube. There are several lava tubes near Bend, Oregon, as well. Exploring these tubes can be fun. You'll need a flashlight, gloves, and a hard hat. If you look along the floor and walls of the tube, you might see little frozen channels where the last remaining lava drained out of the tube. You might also find ice, from water that seeped down into the tube and then froze during the winter. Because of the cool temperatures in the tube, the ice remains all summer.

Clue #3: Rocks And Rock Formations

There are many types of rocks and rock formations that are evidence of volcanic activity. If you look carefully, you might find some.

Volcanic bombs are formed during an eruption. Bits of liquid magma are thrown from the volcano's vent. As they sail through the air like balls, they take on a very spherical (rounded) shape. If they cool enough during their brief flight, they won't splatter when they fall to the ground. Finding a perfectly shaped volcanic bomb can be very

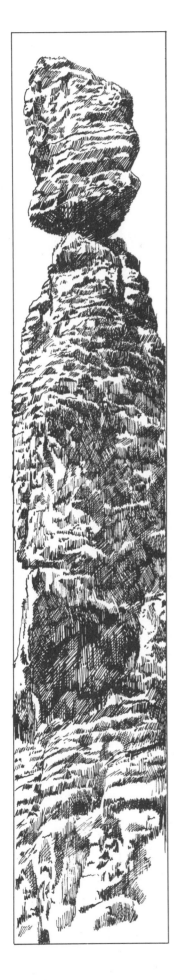

exciting. Don't always think small when looking for these clues—some bombs are over three feet long!

There are other types of rocks and formations that give evidence about volcanic activity. Drop-shaped *lapilli* look like teardrops and are only about one inch long. A volcano may also produce a very fine natural spun glass that looks like fine thread. It trails behind large chunks of magma that are thrown into the air during an eruption, and may float on the wind for miles. *Squeeze-ups* form when lava in a pahoehoe flow squeezes up through cracks in the surface of the lava flow and then cools. They look like black toothpaste that has been squeezed from a tube. Squeeze-ups may be from a few inches to several feet tall.

Geology And Glaciers

Glaciers are master carvers of the Earth's surface. Evidence of glaciers here on Earth can provide tools to detect the presence of water on distant planets.

Here on Earth, glaciers are sometimes called "rivers of ice." They cover about 11 percent of the Earth's land surface, and contain nearly 90 percent of the above–ground water found on Earth. The ice that covers Antarctica is a glacier and is over two miles thick in places. At various times in the past, glaciers covered more of the Earth's surface, and you can still see evidence of that today.

There have been four and perhaps as many as ten glacial advances across the land in the history of the Earth. Sometimes ice came down from the North Pole; sometimes the average temperature dropped enough for glaciers to form in mountain ranges far away from the North Pole. Small parts of glaciers can still be found in mountainous areas.

Glaciers occur when conditions allow ice to form faster than it can melt. When snow falls a long time without melting, the heavy weight of the snow on top gradually compresses the snow beneath it into extremely dense ice. Scientists call this area the *accumulation zone*. The ice becomes so heavy here that it begins to flow downhill under its own weight. It moves down much like thick and cold syrup across a stack of pancakes.

As the heavy river of ice moves downhill, it scrapes up rocks and soil and carries them along. The ice, rocks, and soil grind against everything they touch, scratching and gouging the Earth's surface, carving out valleys. Then the conditions change and the glacial ice melts. The rocks and soil that are left behind show where the glacier stopped. In the glacier's path are new or larger valleys. Scientists call the area where glacial ice melts the *ablation zone*.

You can find evidence of glaciers as you travel around the country. Here are some of the clues that can help tell you the history of the Earth around you.

Clue #1: The Shape Of A Valley

Valleys are usually formed by water, in the form of streams and rivers, or glaciers. Most stream valleys are V-shaped, caused by the downward cutting action of a river or stream. Valleys formed by glaciers, on the other hand, are U-shaped because glacial "rivers" are usually broad rather than narrow.

Clue #2: Scrapes And Scratches

Look for scrapes and scratches on boulders, bedrock, and valley walls. Examine them carefully. They can tell you not only that a glacier passed this way, but the direction in which it was moving. Scientists call these marks *glacial striations*.

Clue #3: Piles Of Rock And Dirt

Piles of jumbled rock and dirt tell you how far a glacier reached before conditions changed and its ice melted. When the ice in a glacier melts, all the rocks and dirt the glacier picked up along the way are left behind, often far from where they started. If you find a rock or boulder that looks very different from the surrounding rock, it might have been put there by a glacier. Sometimes a huge boulder, weighing thousands of tons, has been dropped hundreds of miles from its source by the powerful moving ice of a glacier. Scientists call a boulder such as this a *glacial erractic*.

Using Geological Evidence

Try to find these keys to the geological secrets of the universe as you experience new landscapes here on Earth. In your travels, look for signs of volcanic activity or glaciers. Maybe someday you will be able to use the clues and evidence you gather to help solve the mysteries of places in the solar system we have yet to visit!

Partial List Of Volcanic Areas In Our National Parks

- Capulin Volcano National Monument, New Mexico
- Crater Lake National Park, Oregon
- Devil's Postpile National Monument, California
- Devil's Tower National Monument, Wyoming
- El Malpais National Monument, New Mexico
- Haleakala National Park, Maui, Hawaii
- Hawaii Volcanoes National Park, Hawaii
- Lassen Volcanic National Park, California
- Mount Rainier National Park, Washington
- Sunset Crater Volcano National Monument, Arizona

Partial List Of Glacier Areas In Our National Parks

- Acadia National Park, Maine
- Denali National Park, Alaska
- Glacier Bay National Park and Preserve, Alaska
- Glacier National Park, Montana
- Ice Age Trail, Wisconsin
- Isle Royale National Park, Minnesota
- Mount Rainier National Park, Washington
- North Cascades National Park, Washington
- Rocky Mountain National Park, Colorado
- Yosemite National Park

Suggested Reading

Planet Earth Series by Time-Life, 1982.

Volcano Watching by Robert and Barbara Decker, Hawaii Natural History Association, 1982.

The Thomas A. Jaggar Museum Guidebook by Darcy Bevens and Thomas L. Wright, Hawaii Natural History Association, 1992.

101 Questions about Volcanoes by John Calderazzo, Southwest Parks and Monument Association, 1994.

FIGHTING OVER FOSSILS

by Carolyn Duckworth

Deep within the Grand Canyon, you can find fossils of ancient marine animals called *nautiloids* preserved in the gray rock that overlooks the Colorado River. When you look at them, it's easy to imagine being underwater millions of years ago and watching these creatures swim. These fossils can be seen by anyone willing to scramble up the steep trail. They will always be there because they rest inside Grand Canyon National Park, and collecting fossils without a permit is against the law in all of our national parks. The laws are less clear on other public lands. People who are interested in fossils and who collect them are debating about who should be collecting fossils on these lands and who should own the fossils.

Who Collects Fossils?

Different people collect fossils for different reasons. Some are just interested in them; some are in the business of buying and selling them; and some are scientists who study them.

Amateur Collectors

Amateur collectors are fascinated by ancient life. Often they love searching for fossils as much as they love finding them. They look for fossils on private land and on public land where collecting is allowed. Sometimes they volunteer to help scientists dig for fossils. Most museum fossil collections include fossils found by amateurs. Amateur collectors sometimes sell what they find to other amateurs. But most amateurs keep their fossils, give their fossils to museums, or trade them with other amateurs.

Commercial Collectors

Commercial collectors may have started collecting fossils for fun, but now they collect for money—big money. A finely detailed plant fossil might sell for a hundred dollars or more. A beautiful fish fossil can sell for a thousand dollars. Any fossil from a dinosaur can sell for many thousands— even millions—of dollars. Commercial collectors often pay private landowners for the right to collect or dig for fossils on their property. They can also apply for permits to collect certain kinds of fossils from some public lands, such as those managed by the U.S. Forest Service or the Bureau of Land Management. But they cannot sell the fossils they collect on those lands.

Paleontologists

Paleontologists are scientists who study fossils in order to learn about plants and animals that lived long ago. They look for fossils of dinosaurs, fish, mammals, plants, and even organisms so small that you can see them only under a microscope. In recent years, some paleontologists have specialized in studying entire ecosystems. For this branch of paleontology, called *paleoecology,* scientists need to study all the fossils found in an area. Every item is important because it is a clue that can help tell the story of life at a particular place on Earth in the past.

Paleontologists often work for museums and universities that do not have the money to pay for the right to collect fossils from private lands. Instead, they apply for permits to collect on public lands. Any fossils they find are studied, stored, and often displayed in museums that are open to the public. All the fossils they collect on public land remain the property of the United States.

Are They Fighting?

The question of who should be able to collect fossils and who owns them seems to start with a conflict between science and money. In the 1990s, public interest in fossils has grown beyond anyone's wildest dreams. You can buy fossils in "nature" stores, from catalogs, and even on the Internet. Fossils are bought, sold, and traded at mineral and gem shows and by mail around the country and around the world. Every year thousands of fossils found in the United States, including entire dinosaur skeletons, end up in private homes and museums in other countries.

Our knowledge of ancient life has expanded dramatically because paleontologists have been able to study fossils closely. They carefully scrape and chisel and then gently remove thousands of bones and fragments. They keep detailed notes about each item—where it was found, what it was near. When the digging is done, scientists use their knowledge and training to figure out what these particular fossils in this particular place tell us about life in the past.

What do you think happens when an important fossil site is found by someone interested only in making money and who knows that one dinosaur egg can sell for several thousand dollars? Some commercial collectors donate scientifically important fossils to scientists, but others choose to sell the fossils for a lot of money. Not many scientists or museums can afford to pay high prices for fossils at auctions and at gem and mineral shows. Once the fossil leaves the country or is bought by a private collector, it cannot be reexamined or studied by other researchers. It is lost forever.

Commercial collectors point out that if fossils aren't collected, they will be lost to science anyway. They claim that, especially in the western United States, millions of fossils are lost each year because water and wind destroy them. Scientists say that this is not necessarily true. Destruction by wind and water takes a very long time. Amateur and professional paleontologists could search most of these areas often enough to recover many fossils before they are destroyed. Paleontologists also explain that fossils are just as lost if they are collected and sold without ever being examined by scientists.

There is also a debate over who should be allowed to collect on public lands. The Bureau of Land Management and the U.S. Forest Service now allow people to collect plant and invertebrate fossils (fossils of animals without backbones) from the Earth's surface without a permit. People need permits to collect vertebrate fossils or to dig beneath the surface. Other U.S. government agencies have different policies. Although laws have been proposed several times to create uniform rules, none has been passed. Some paleontologists say that a uniform collecting policy probably isn't possible because so many kinds of fossils exist, there are lots of some kinds and few of others, and their scientific value varies. Meanwhile, none of the agencies has enough money to pay people to look at permits and supervise collecting on millions of acres of undeveloped land in the western United States.

Why not just let commercial and amateur collectors loose on public lands? That's probably not a wise way to ensure that important fossils are saved and turned over to science. Commercial collectors say that they would call a professional paleontologist to evaluate fossils that seem important; but not all commercial collectors know enough about fossils to understand what is important. Amateurs do not always understand the importance of what they've found, either. Sometimes, they pick up a sliver of bone and don't realize that the fragment is the only clue to an entire skeleton or large group of bones beneath the surface. Commercial and amateur collectors also may not take detailed notes of where they found an important fossil. When that happens, paleontologists can't go back to find out what else is in the area. Careless collection like this can be more damaging to our understanding of past life than the loss of fossils to natural forces.

Perhaps the most difficult question is who should own fossils collected on public lands—land that everyone in the United States owns. Some of the proposed laws allow individuals to own fossils they find on public land. This idea is strongly supported by many commercial collectors, who could then sell fossils they find on public land. A survey conducted in 1995 asked the general public about this issue. More than 80 percent of the people who answered the survey said they believe that fossils found on public land should belong to the public, they should not be sold, and they should remain in the United States.

Sharing The Wealth

The United States contains millions of fossils. Some are on private land and are available to scientific, commercial, and amateur collectors with the landowners' permission. Some are in national parks where we all can admire and inspect them. Some are on other public lands where collectors must prove that they know what they are doing and must promise that the fossils will remain public property in the United States and will be stored properly.

These rules are still being debated. Do they seem unfair? Should we open our public lands to unsupervised collecting? Should we allow fossils from our public lands to be sold to the highest bidder? As you think about how you would answer these questions, remember that paleontologists who collect from public lands share what they find with all of us. As they study fossils and piece together the story of ancient life, they tell us about their discoveries through teaching, magazine articles, films, and museum exhibits. If fossils are sold to the highest bidder, most of us will never have a chance to see what we've lost.

FOSSIL FORUM: WHAT WOULD YOU DO?

by Carolyn Duckworth

T he issue of fossil collecting is one that provides many ideas for classroom activities and investigations. You can find plenty of current information on the Internet from commercial collectors, amateur collectors, and professional paleontologists. (Be aware, though, that much misinformation exists on the Internet, too.)

Look at the public poll that follows. Do the questions seem fair? Do they seem to lead to one answer or another?

Conduct the fossil poll in your school. Compile the answers and discuss the results.

The Purpose And Results Of The Poll

This poll was conducted because the paleontological community wanted to find out how the people of the United States feel about commercial collecting of fossils on public lands. (See "Fighting Over Fossils.")

The Poll

The poll consists of three scenarios—brief stories, each describing a situation involving finding fossils on public or private land. After reading each scenario, people are asked whether they agree or disagree with several statements. Their answers reveal their attitudes and opinions about collecting fossils in the situation described. The scenarios are designed to reveal differences in attitudes about fossils of vertebrates (animals with backbones) and invertebrates (animals without backbones), differences in attitudes about fossils on private and public land, as well as other attitudes and opinions about collecting fossils.

Scenario #1

Imagine that you have inherited a large ranch out West. On a visit to your ranch, you discover the fossil bones of an animal. At first you think that they are the bones of a cow that died in recent years. However, on closer inspection you find that the bones are stone, the skull is strange-looking, and the backbone looks different from anything you've seen. Pieces of bone are washing out of a rock ledge; they are falling apart and appear very fragile. You recall that someone told you that the fossil bones of ancient creatures, millions of years old, are sometimes found in the area.

Remember, you own the ranch.

Scenario #2

After your discovery, you obtain a detailed survey of your property. You find out that you had actually wandered off of your property and onto public property—part of a national grasslands, a federal wilderness area, or a national park. The fossil is not on your land after all; it is on these public lands.

Scenario #3

Imagine you are on another visit to the ranch. Again you wander off the ranch onto public property—part of a national grasslands, a federal wilderness area, or a national park. This time you discover the fossils of animals without backbones. Some look like crabs, some like corals, and others are unlike anything you have ever seen. The rock seems loaded with their impressions. You recall that someone told you that the fossils of these strange creatures, millions of years old, are sometimes found in the area.

Remember, you are on public property.

Questions

These are the questions to ask people after they have read (or you have read to them) each scenario. Reproduce this form and use it to record each person's answers. Check "Agree" or "Disagree" for each question regarding each scenario.

Scenario Questions

	SCENARIO 1 Vertebrate/ Private	SCENARIO 2 Vertebrate/ Public	SCENARIO 3 Invertebrate/ Public

Q1 The fossil is mine; finders keepers.

Agree	Agree	Agree
Disagree	Disagree	Disagree

Q2 The fossil could be of scientific importance. I should report it to appropriate scientific authorities.

Agree	Agree	Agree
Disagree	Disagree	Disagree

Q3 The fossil could be of scientific importance. If they want it, I should allow a museum or university to collect it.

Agree	Agree	Agree
Disagree	Disagree	Disagree

Q4 The fossil is part of our heritage; it belongs to everyone in the United States.

Agree	Agree	Agree
Disagree	Disagree	Disagree

Q5 The fossil is on my property. I should be allowed to do whatever I want with it. That's my right, and that's what matters most.

Agree	Agree	Agree
Disagree	Disagree	Disagree

Q6 There should be a law that says I can't take the fossil out of the ground.

Agree	Agree	Agree
Disagree	Disagree	Disagree

Q7 There should be a law against my selling the fossil.

Agree	Agree	Agree
Disagree	Disagree	Disagree

Q8 There should be a law against my taking the fossil out of the United States.

Agree	Agree	Agree
Disagree	Disagree	Disagree

GENERAL QUESTIONS

Q1 It's okay with me for someone to buy and sell fossils.

       Agree   Disagree

Q2 Fossils found on public lands should be restricted. It should be illegal to collect them, to sell them, to destroy them, to export them out of the United States.

       Agree   Disagree

Q3 Fossils found on private land should be legally available for sale.

       Agree   Disagree

Q4 All fossils found in the United States, whether found on private or public lands, should be the property of public institutions like museums or universities.

       Agree   Disagree

Q5 There should be a law to stop people from collecting fossils on federally managed public lands.

       Agree   Disagree

Q6 There should be a law to stop people from collecting fossils on all state lands.

       Agree   Disagree

Q7a Fossils of animals with backbones are part of our national heritage and should be protected the same way that archeological remains (human artifacts) are now protected.

       Agree   Disagree

Q7b Fossils of animals without backbones are part of our national heritage and should be protected the same way that archeological remains (human artifacts) are now protected.

       Agree   Disagree

Q8 This is the United States. We should encourage free enterprise. A law against selling fossils collected on private lands is wrong.

       Agree   Disagree

Q9 If someone finds a fossil of a dinosaur and wants to keep it in his or her basement, that's fine with me.

       Agree   Disagree

Q10 If someone finds a fossil of a dinosaur, he or she should not remove without help from professionals or scientists.

       Agree   Disagree

Q11 If laws are passed to restrict the collection of fossils on public lands, the only people who should be allowed to collect them are people with appropriate skills for doing so and with a permit. All the fossils that they find should go into museums or universities prepared to protect them.

       Agree   Disagree

Q12 Fossils bring big money these days. People should be allowed to buy and sell them just like any other product.

       Agree   Disagree

© The Society of Vertebrate Paleontology

85

What Does The Poll Tell You?

After you have everyone's answers to the questions, count how many people answered "Agree" and "Disagree" to each question. Then use the results to summarize people's attitudes and opinions about collecting and selling fossils.

Note to Teachers: This article is most appropriate for grades 4 to 8. However, after reviewing it, you may decide to share it with your younger students either by reading aloud or paraphrasing.

mammoth

Bibliography Update

Note: A * at the end of a listing indicates that the book is a good source of geology pictures.

GENERAL REFERENCE BOOKS

Agents of Change by Stephen L. Harris (Mountain Press Publishing Co., 1994) *

Continents in Motion: The New Earth Debate by Walter Sullivan (American Institute of Physics, 1991)

Crystal and Gems by R.F. Symes (Dorling Kindersley, 1993) *

Crystals and Crystal Growing by Alan Holden and Phylis Morrison (MIT, 1982)

Dictionary of the Earth by John Farndon (Dorling Kindersley, 1995)

Earth by Susanna Van Rose (Dorling Kindersley, 1994) Part of the Eyewitness Science Series.

The Earth Atlas by Susanna Van Rose (Dorling Kindersley, 1994)

Earthquakes and Geological Discovery by Bruce A. Bolt (Scientific American Library, 1993) *

Encyclopedia of Earthquakes and Volcanoes by David Rithie (Facts on File, 1994)

Ever Since Darwin: Reflections in Natural History by Stephen Jay Gould (W.W. Norton and Co., 1977)

Fossils: The Key to the Past by Richard Fortey (Van Nostrand Reinhold, 1982) *

Giants from the Past (National Geographic Society, 1983)

Ice Ages: Solving the Mystery by John Imbrie and Katherine Palmer Imbrie (Harvard University Press, 1994)

Mountains by Jack D. Ives (Rodale Press, 1994) *

Mountains and Plains: The Ecology of Wyoming Landscapes by Dennis H. Knight (Yale University Press, 1994)

Naked Earth: The New Geophysics by Shawna Vogel (A Dutton Book, 1995)

Nature on the Rampage (National Geographic Society, 1994)

Physical Geography of the Global Environment by H.J. de Blij and Peter O. Muller (John Wiley and Sons, 1993) *

Planet Ocean: A Story of Life, the Sea, and Dancing to the Fossil Record by Brad Matsen (Ten Speed Press, 1994) *

Shaping the Earth: Tectonics of Continents and Oceans by Eldridge M. Morris (W.H. Truman and Co., 1990)

A Short History of Planet Earth: Mountains, Mammals, Fire and Ice by J.D. MacDougall (John Wiley and Sons, 1996)

Volcanoes of North America: U.S. and Canada edited by Charles A. Wood and Jürgen Kienle (Cambridge University Press, 1990) *

Water, Stones, and Fossil Bones: Earth Science Activities for Elementary and Middle Level Grades edited by Karen K. Lind (CESI Sourcebook VI, 1991, Council for Elementary Science International and National Science Teachers Association)

FIELD GUIDES

A Field Guide to Rocks and Minerals by Frederick H. Pough (Houghton Mifflin, 1995). This is part of the Peterson Field Guide Series.

Audubon Society Field Guide to North American Rocks and Minerals by Charles W. Chesterman (Alfred A. Knopf, 1995)

Audubon Society Pocket Guides, Familiar Fossils in North America (Alfred A. Knopf, 1988)

Audubon Society Pocket Guides, Familiar Rocks and Minerals (Alfred A. Knopf, 1988)

Dinosaur Safari Guide: Tracking North America's Prehistoric Past by Vincent Corta (Voyageur Press, Inc., 1994)

A Field Manual for the Amateur Geologist by Alan M. Cvancara (John Wiley and Sons, 1995). Advanced *

Fossils by Frank H. T. Rhodes (Golden, 1962) *

Peterson First Guide, Rocks and Minerals by Frederick H. Plough (Houghton Mifflin, 1991)

Rocks and Minerals by Charles Sorrell (Golden, 1973)

CHILDREN'S BOOKS

Adventures with Rocks and Minerals, Book II: Geology Experiments for Young People by Lloyd H. Barrow (Enslow, 1995). Intermediate/Advanced

After the Ice Age: The Return of Life to Glaciated North America by E.C. Pielou (University of Chicago Press, 1991). Advanced

The Big Rock by Bruce Hiscock (Atheneum Books Young, 1988). Primary

Book of Planet Earth by Martyn Bramwell (Simon & Schuster Books for Young Readers, 1992). Intermediate *

Blue Planet by Barbara Hehner (Gulliver Books, 1992). Intermediate *

A Children's Guide to Dinosaurs and Other Prehistoric Animals by Philip Whitfield (MacMillan Publishing, 1992). Primary/Intermediate

Crystal and Gems by R.F. Symes (Knopf, 1991). Advanced *

Crystals by Ian F. Mercer (Harvard University Press, 1990). Advanced *

Death Trap: The Story of the La Brea Tar Pit by Sharon Elaine Thompson (Lerner Publications Co., 1995). Intermediate

Digging Deeper: Investigations into Rocks, Shocks, Quakes and Other Earthy Matters by Sandra Markle (Lothrop, Lee & Shepard, 1987). Intermediate/Advanced

Dinosaur Tree by Douglas Henderson (Bradbury Press, 1994). Primary/Intermediate *

Earth by Iqbal Hussain (Thomson Learning, 1995). Intermediate

The Earth and How It Works by Steve Parker is part of the See & Explore Library series. (Dorling Kindersley, 1992). Intermediate/Advanced

Earth and Other Planets: Geology and Space Research by Peter Cattermole (Oxford University Press, 1995). Advanced *

Earth Facts by Cally Hall and Scarlett O'Hara (Dorling Kindersley, 1995). Advanced

The Earth: Origins and Evolution by Anna Alessandrello (Raintree, 1994). Intermediate/Advanced

The Earth Pack: Tornadoes, Earthquakes, Volcanoes, Nature's Forces in Three Dimensions by Ron van der Mier and Ron Fisher (National Geographic Society, 1995). With sound effects. Primary *

The Earth Science Book Activities for Kids by Dinah Zike (John Wiley and Sons, 1993). Intermediate

Earth Science: Discovering Basic Concepts (Janus Books, 1987). Primary/Intermediate *

Earth's Surface by Jon Erikson (Facts on File, 1993). Advanced

Earthquakes by Seymour Simon (Morrow Junior Books, 1991). Primary/Intermediate

Earthquakes and Volcanoes by Basil Booth (Mac Books for Young Readers, 1991/1992). Intermediate

Everybody Needs a Rock by Byrd Baylor (Aladdin Books, MacMillan Publishing, 1985). Primary

Fossil Identifier by Scott Weidensaul (Mallard Press, 1992). Advanced *

Fossils: A Guide to Prehistoric Life by Frank H.T. Rhodes (Golden Press, 1962) *

Geology (Golden Press, 1991). Intermediate/Advanced *

Geology by Graham Peacock and Jill Jesson (Thomson Learning, 1995). Primary

Glaciers by Michael Hambrey (Cambridge University Press, 1992). Advanced *

Gold! The True Story of Why People Search for It, Mine It, Trade It, Steal It, Mint It, Shape It, Wear It, Fight and Kill for It by Milton Meltzer (HarperCollins Children's Books, 1993). Intermediate

Handbook of Rocks, Minerals and Gemstones by Walter Schumann (Houghton Mifflin, 1993). Advanced *

Hands-on Elementary School Science: Earth Science by Linda Poore (1994). Activity binder. Primary/Intermediate

How Mountains Are Made by Kathleen Weidner Zoehfield (HarperCollins, 1995). Primary

I Can Be a Geologist by Paul P. Sipiera (Children's Press, 1986). Primary *

Icebergs: Titans of the Oceans by Jenny Wood (Gareth Stevens Children's Books, 1991). Primary/Intermediate

The Illustrated Dictionary of Earth Sciences (Bloomsbury Books, 1994). Intermediate *

Imprints of Time: The Art of Geology by Bradford B. Van Dever (Montana Press Co., 1988). Advanced *

An Introduction to Fossils and Minerals: Seeking Clues to Earth's Past by Jon Erickson (Facts on File, 1992). Advanced *

The Magic School Bus in the Time of the Dinosaurs by Joanna Cole (Scholastic Inc., 1994). Primary *

The Magic School Bus Inside the Earth by Joanna Cole (Scholastic, Inc., 1987). Primary

Mineral Resources by Robin Kerrod (Thomson Learning, 1994). Intermediate/Advanced

Mountains by Neil Morris (Crabtree Publishing, 1996). Primary/Intermediate

Mountains by Seymour Simon (Morrow Junior Books, 1994). Primary/ intermediate

Mountains and Volcanoes by Barbara Taylor (Kingfisher Books, 1992/1993). Primary

Natural Wonders and Disasters by Billy Goodman (Little, Brown & Co., 1991). Intermediate/Advanced

Our Planet Earth by Isaac Asimov and Francis Reddy (Gareth Stevens, 1995). Intermediate

Our Planet Earth by Steve Parker (Facts on File, 1994). Intermediate/Advanced

Our Planet: Volcanoes and Earthquakes by Zuza Vrbova (Eagle Books Limited, 1990). Intermediate

Our Restless Earth by Roy A. Gallant (Franklin Watts, 1986). Primary *

Planet Earth Inside Out by Gail Gibbons (Morrow Junior Books, 1995). Primary/Intermediate

Powerful Waves by Dorothy M. Souza (Carolrhoda Books, 1992). Primary/Intermediate *

The Practical Geologist by Dougal Dixon (Simon & Schuster, 1992). Intermediate/Advanced *

The Practical Paleontologist by Steve Parker (Simon & Schuster, 1990). Intermediate/Advanced *

Quake by Joe Cottonwood (Scholastic Inc., 1995). Intermediate

Quakes, Eruptions and Other Geologic Cataclysms by Jon Erickson (Facts on File, 1994). Advanced *

Roadside Geology is a series with books covering many states. (Mountain Press Publishing Co., 1975-1991). Intermediate/Advanced

Rock Formations and Unusual Geologic Structures: Exploring the Earth's Surface by Jon Erickson (Facts on File, 1993). Advanced *

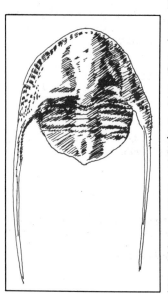

Rocks and Fossils by Marilyn Bramwell (EDC Publishing, 1994). Primary

Rocks and Minerals by Joel Arem (Geoscience Press, 1991). Advanced *

Rocks and Minerals by Sue Fuller is part of the Pockets Full of Knowledge series. (Dorling Kindersley, 1995). Advanced

Rocks and Minerals by Keith Lye (Raintree-Steck-Vaughn Co., 1993). Primary *

Rocks and Minerals by Chris Pellant (Dorling Kindersley, 1992). Intermediate/Advanced *

Rocks and Minerals by R.F. Symmes (Alfred A. Knopf, 1988). Intermediate *

Rocks and Minerals: Mind Boggling Experiments You Can Turn into Science Fair Projects by Janice Van Cleave (John Wiley and Sons, 1996). Primary/Intermediate

Rocks and Soil by Joy Richardson (Franklin Watts, 1992). Primary

Rocks Tell Stories by Sidney S. Horenstein (Millbrook Press, 1993). Intermediate

Simon & Schuster's Young Readers' Book of Planet Earth by Martyn Bramwell (Simon & Schuster Books for Young Readers, 1992). Intermediate *

Storms by Seymour Simon (Morrow Juvenile Books, 1989). Primary/Intermediate *

Time, Rocks and the Rockies by Halka Chronic (Mountain Press Publishing Co., 1984). Advanced *

The Visual Dictionary of the Earth (Dorling Kindersley, 1993). Intermediate *

Volcanoes by Neil Morris (Crabtree Publishing, 1996). Primary/Intermediate

Volcanoes by Seymour Simon (Morrow Mulberry, 1988). Primary *

Volcano: The Eruption of Mount St. Helens by Patricia Lauber (Bradbury Press, 1986). Intermediate/Advanced *

Volcanoes and Earthquakes by Eldridge M. Moores (Time-Life Books, 1995). Intermediate/Advanced

Volcanoes & Earthquakes by Susanna Van Rose (Knopf, 1992) Intermediate/Advanced *

Where to Find Dinosaurs Today by Daniel and Susan Cohen (Cobblehill Books, 1992). Intermediate

CD-ROM AND COMPUTER SOFTWARE

Geology (Grades 4–9) is part of National Geographic Society PictureShow CD-ROMs series (National Geographic, 1994). To order, write to:
National Geographic Society
Educational Services
P.O. Box 98018
Washington, DC, 20090-8018
U.S.A.
or call:
1-800-368-2728

Red Shift 2 by Maris Multimedia and distributed by Maxis, 1994–1995. For more information contact:
Maris Multimedia
4040 Civic Center Drive, Ste. 200
San Rafael, CA 94903
U.S.A.
or call:
415-492-2819

Contact Maxis at:
2121 North California Blvd., Ste 600
Walnut Creek, CA 94596
U.S.A.
or call:
510-933-5630

VIDEO, FILMSTRIPS AND OTHER EDUCATIONAL RESOURCES

Every Stone Has a Story (Grades 4–9) by National Geographic, 1995.

Exploring the Earth Around Us (Grades 3–5) by National Geographic, 1993. 5 episodes: Mountains, Deserts, Oceans, Plains, Rivers.

The Forces of Nature, Weather, Floods, and Forest Fires, Volcanoes and Earthquakes (Grades 4–9) by National Geographic, 1993.

Hidden Fury: The New Madrid Earthquake (Grades 7 and up) by Bullfrog Films, 1993. To order, write to:
Bullfrog Films
P.O. Box 149
Oley, PA 19547
U.S.A.

or call
1-800-543-3764

Our Dynamic Earth (Grades 7–12) by National Geographic, 1979.

Ranger Rick's® Science Spectacular: Remarkable Rocks (Grades 2–4) by Newbridge Communications, 1996. To order, fax Newbridge at: 212-455-5750

Volcano by National Geographic, 1992. To order, write to:
National Geographic Society
Educational Services
P.O. Box 98018
Washington, DC 20090-8018
U.S.A.

or call:
1-800-368-2728

What's the Earth Made Of? (Grades 4–9) by National Geographic, 1995.

BOOKLETS, KITS, MAPS

American Geological Institute has books and pamphlets on many geology topics. For more information write:
American Geological Institute
4220 King St.
Alexandria, VA 22302
U.S.A.

Massachusetts Audubon Society. Write for catalog of materials.
Massachusetts Audubon Society Educational Resources
208 S. Great Rd.
Lincoln, MA 01773
U.S.A.

National Geographic Society has topographic and satellite image maps of the Grand Canyon, the United States, and the Americas. For more information write:
National Geographic Society
Educational Services
Dept. 85
Washington, DC 20036
U.S.A.

U.S. Geological Survey has many pamphlets, books, maps, lists of resources, and a "Selected Packet of Geologic Teaching Aids," among other items. For more information write:
U.S. Geological Survey
Geologic Inquiries Group
907 National Center
Reston, VA 22092
U.S.A.

OTHER ACTIVITY SOURCES

American Coal Foundation. For more information write:
American Coal Foundation
1130 17th Street, Suite 220
Washington, DC 20036
U.S.A.

National Earth Science Teachers Association has a journal, *The Earth Scientist* and short slide sets appropriate for advanced groups. For more information write:
NESTA
c/o Frank Ireton
2000 Florida Ave N.W.
Washington, DC 20009
U.S.A.

WHERE TO GET ROCK AND MINERAL SAMPLES

Carolina Biological Supply Company has rock and mineral samples, fossils, and other geology materials. For more information write:
Carolina Biological Supply Company
2700 York Rd.
Burlington, NC 27215
U.S.A.

or call:
1-800-334-5551

Delta Education has rock and mineral samples, crystal-growing kits, charts, and guides. For more information write:
Delta Education
P.O. Box M
Nashua, NH 03061-6012
U.S.A.

Ward's Natural Science Establishment has rock and mineral samples, fossils, and many other materials. For more information write:
Ward's Natural Science Establishment, Inc.
5100 Henrietta Rd.
P.O. Box 92912
Rochester, NY 14692-9012
U.S.A.

or call:
1-800-962-2660

WHERE TO GET MORE INFORMATION

- college and university departments of geology
- museums
- nature centers
- rock and mineral clubs
- U.S. Geological Survey. Geologic Inquiries Group, 907 National Center, Reston, VA 22092
- World Wide Web sites:
  U.S. Fish and Wildlife Service can be reached at http://www.fws.gov
  U.S. Geological Survey can be reached at http://www.usgs.gov

Internet Address Disclaimer
The Internet information provided here was correct, to the best of our knowledge, at the time of publication. It is important to remember, however, the dynamic nature of the Internet. Resources that are free and publicly available one day may require a fee or restrict access the next, and the location of items may change as menus and homepages are reorganized.